# UNLEASH
## *the*
# LEADER
## *within*
# YOU!

# HOW TO ACHIEVE THE SUCCESS THAT YOU DESERVE

# UNLEASH
## *the*
# LEADER
## *within*
# YOU!

# HOW TO ACHIEVE
# THE SUCCESS THAT
# YOU DESERVE

*Chip Cummings • Cy Forh • Dave Sheffield • Dawn Strozier*
*Greg Cook • Hassan Omar • Lisa Panarello • Matt Kuennen*
*Robin Aikens • Rosa Williams Sherk • Shanita Akintonde*
*Stephanie Durden • Stephen Duncanson • Kevin Bracy*
*James Malinchak*

Printed in the United States of America

ISBN# 0-9769905-8-X

Cover Graphics by Dawn Teagarden — dteagarden@earthlink.net

Warning – Disclaimer
The purpose of this book is to educate and entertain. The authors or publisher does not guarantee that anyone following the ideas, tips, suggestions, techniques or strategies will become successful. The authors and publisher shall have neither liability or responsibility to anyone with respect to any loss or damage caused, or alleged to be caused, directly or indirectly by the information contained in this book.

# Table of Contents

## Chip Cummings

Chip Cummings is a nationally recognized speaker and author in the field of technology marketing, addressing thousands of executives and sales professionals each year at various conventions and meetings around the world. Since starting his own corporation at the age of 15, he has held the position of CEO, President, has been on the Board of Directors of several different companies and associations, and racked up over $1 Billion in sales volume.

Chip is a recipient of the MMBA Leadership Award, and numerous other state and national awards for his work in the areas of corporate and executive development, e-marketing strategies, and industry education. He is the author of several books, including **"Stop Selling and Start Listening! – Marketing Strategies That Create Top Producers"** and is a regular columnist for several national publications.

Currently, Chip spends most of his time consulting and speaking to corporations and business organizations on developing creative ways to attract, capture, convert and retain customers. His client list includes notables such as GMAC, First Franklin, Les Brown, AT&T, General Electric, Ellie Mae, and Patriot National Bank.

He currently resides in Rockford, Michigan with his wife Lisa and three children, Katelyn, C.J. and Joe.

**Chip Cummings**
137 Pearl St. NW, Suite 400
Grand Rapids, MI  49503

(866) 977-7900

www.ChipCummings.com

# 7 Rules That Create Effective Leaders

You've heard people say it a thousand times – "He's a natural born leader" or "He was born to lead!" It's as if they believe leaders were given a genetic "leg up" in the same way Michael Jordan was born with certain advantages to play basketball. Hogwash!

I don't believe this. Unlike basketball, where some natural-born talent is the minimum admission to a professional sports career, effective leadership is a learned skill. In other words, "Leaders" don't have better genes than you – they have just learned and developed more effective habits.

## Successful Habits of Effective Leadership

After working with and studying the habits of thousands of successful producers, and analyzing their habits and methods of success, I've boiled their formula down to something I call *"Chip's Seven Rules for Success."* When building and leading a successful organization, it helps if you have certain guideposts along the way. So, the seven rules are in order, starting with those tasks you need to concentrate on first, as if you are starting from ground zero. Some of these rules could easily fill an entire separate book on the subject, but we'll cover them as completely as possible.

## 1. Rule of Reality

This is the "You Are Here" arrow for your business. When you're starting a journey, you need to know where you are first, before you can begin to map

where it is you want to go. This rule establishes where you are NOW. Leaders are able to clearly define themselves and what they do before they start their success journey.

*To truly get a fix on your current location, you'll need to ask yourself these questions*:

- What is your Unique Value Proposition (UVP)?
- Can you clearly define your "Personal Value" in seven seconds?
- Who is your direct target audience or "perfect" customer?
- What is your business plan to reach that target audience?
- What marketing and sales systems will you use?
- What are my strategies for communicating these to my team?
- What are my current limitations for leading my team to success?

## 2. Rule of Reach

Once you determine where you are and have identified your goals, your next task is to establish the rules of the road and set up a system for reaching customers.

You will start by thoroughly researching exactly what it is your target market "and your team members" want. You will quickly learn that you cannot serve everyone, so you must segment the market and decide where you will concentrate your main efforts. Who are the customers you will serve? What is their niche? Where exactly do we find them? Can you lead your team to the target market?

Then you need to react to your research. You will discover ways to analyze and target the Suspects, and develop appropriate solutions to reach them. All of your internal systems and marketing strategies need to revolve around establishing a "relational" rather than a "transactional" customer experience. Your goal is to establish a "business friendship", and position yourself as a trustworthy and reliable expert resource which satisfies their need for information – someone who exhibits a desire for future, repeat business through concern for *their* interests. This "relationship" strategy must then be a "core" part of your teams delivery process of your products and services.

Finally, you need to learn to "respect" your customers and your team members by not *selling* to them, but rather *listening* to them. For your team members, you will need to establish a system and plan where your team can regularly contact Prospects six or seven times without applying the "hard sell." Through database tracking systems, you'll need to organize your customers into three types: past (customers who may purchase with you again), present (customers you are actively servicing now), and future (new customers with which you are trying to connect). Rather than focusing on just your services and products, you need to help your team decide what experience you want all your customers to have when they come in contact with your company and team members. Once you have mastered The Rule of Reach, you and your team will start filling your client list with laser-targeted, qualified Prospects.

## 3. Rule of Restlessness

Leaders don't rest. Everyone only has 24 hours in a day, but Leaders have figured out how to work smarter, not harder. They leverage technology and spend a lot of time fine tuning their systems. They are never 100% satisfied with their marketing systems and internal team resources, and are constantly looking for ways to make them more effective. Complacency is not in their vocabulary, and they have an insatiable appetite for learning new ways to sharpen their skills. Remember, a sharp axe will cut down a tree in less time than a dull one, and if I only have 20 hours to cut it down, I'll spend 17 of those hours sharpening my axe. Spend more time sharpening your own axe. Constantly test different systems and track the results to make sure your operation is running at peak efficiency, and never become satisfied with the status quo.

Effective leaders also recognize that the path to success doesn't come by accident – it comes through education. They know firsthand that education can only be obtained in one of two ways: either through making mistakes or by tapping into resources that illustrate the experiences of others to avoid mistakes. Invest in the best resources you can find, including educational materials and professional coaching. Every leader has a mentor, or someone who can identify their strengths and weaknesses, and keeps them focused on driving down the right road. Always be researching ways to avoid mistakes – it's much cheaper.

## 4. Rule of Retention

Leaders know how to provide a first-class experience for their customers and team members. They consistently under-promise and over-deliver. Mastery of this Rule will make you stand out from average operations who do just the opposite – the ones who over-promise and under-deliver! Not that they try to, but they end up promising the world just to get the sale, and then have to work twice as hard to live up to the expectation. If you promise eight things and only deliver seven, the team and your customers will remember the one thing you missed! On the other hand, if you promise eight things and deliver ten, statistics show that they're going to tell an average of eight people about the "over-the-top" service you provided and what an enjoyable experience it was to work with you and to be a part of your team. If you fall short, they'll tell 20.

Go the extra mile to create the "WOW" effect for your customers, and turn them into Evangelists. For example, I had a client that was short one document for his real estate closing. I could have just said, "OK, just mail it and we'll delay the closing for another day or two," but I told him not to worry, I would take care of it. So, I drove one hour out of my way just to get the last document we needed to finish the closing. The customer was amazed and called to tell me that "no one else he knew would do that for him." Within the next six months, he referred five other customers to us. More importantly, my employees and "team members" took note and strived to deliver that level of service.

## 5. Rule of Referrals

For Leaders, referrals are the life-blood of future success. You do not have enough time, money, energy or resources to invest in the creation of a new customer or team member every time you need to generate income. You will either go broke or become a victim of "burn-out."

Research shows that, for every dollar you spend retaining an existing team member, you'll spend eleven dollars trying to get a new one. Leaders have systems for maintaining contact with their team members and customers on a regular basis and creating an environment which encourages referrals. Known as DRIP marketing systems, these database and customer relationship management programs automate the process of relationship-building.

Train your team members to wait until after the sale to ask for referrals. The process starts at the very beginning of the relationship. Teach them to set the stage right at the start by indicating that they primarily work from a referral base, because you enjoy working with friends and associates of happy customers. I was recently asked by a reporter how much of my business was from referrals, and I indicated that it was over 95%. He was shell-shocked! "How can that be?" he asked.

First, I've been doing this for many years, and have built up a pretty good bank of clients. But more than that, I have a system and I teach that system to all my team members. I have a system that has been fine-tuned so well that it works automatically – with or without me. I explained how I have reached the point in my professional career where I really get to "pick and choose" who I work with, and that I do it for the love of it – not the money. He understood the power of this completely different approach.

I have a detailed training program called managing success from the inside-out which looks at how to develop and implement a dynamic internal referral system. Soon to be released in an upcoming book, this process provides the blueprint for creating an automatic, repeatable yet simple system for maintaining team members, and how to capitalize on the "lifetime value of the environment."

Another way to keep referrals coming in for your newer salespeople is to teach them how to simply keep in touch with their customers! A 2002 study of customers who had gone through the sales process revealed that 90% of the customers contacted could not remember after one year who their sales person was! They might remember the company, but usually not the individual. Don't let this happen to you! You need to create a system which "touches" a customer at least four to six times a year just to remind them who you are. How do you do this? Some examples include phone calls, e-mails, free reports, article clippings, e-zines, direct mail information pieces, holiday cards, tele-conferences, or using an automated DRIP system – just to name a few!

## 6. Rule of Relationships

Leaders know how to nurture both internal and external relationships, and take care of key people in critical areas of support. Internal relationships include your team of employees, assistants, business and internal systems partners. There is an enormous value in creating a close-knit internal support community that you can trust and depend on, and it goes way beyond what money can buy. Treat these support people like gold. Make sure that everyone in the support system, from your top salesperson right down to your receptionist, knows your dreams, goals and business plan. When everyone is "in sync" working towards the same end, the results come faster, problems get solved quicker, and the bonds become almost unbreakable. Simple things matter, and may take the form of occasional pizza parties or casual Fridays. However you do it, make sure the people you work with understand that they are an important piece of the success puzzle, and that you take the time to share your organization's success with them.

While this type of internal community is vital for success, it is also relatively rare. Those of you who have witnessed this know what I mean, and understand the magic effect this can have in an organization. Leaders know this as well, and strive to put the right players in key spots, and take very good care of them in many ways.

Your Key – External relationships include customers and affiliate partners. I've already touched on how to take care of customer relationships in Rules four and five. Affiliate partners include anyone who supports the customer transaction outside of your organization. This can include vendors, retailers, wholesalers, and professionals providing complementary services which benefit YOUR client base. For example, in the mortgage industry there are real estate agents, builders, title companies, appraisers, certified financial planners, CPAs, and tax attorneys.

Make sure you seek out well qualified, top-notch professionals, and establish a win-win relationship with these parties. One way you can do this is to embark on some "fusion marketing" with some key players. For example, in the mortgage industry, I might target first-time home buyers as my primary customer market. Who do I know that deals directly with first-time home buyers? Real estate agents. So, I will approach real estate agents who deal with homes in the market range of a typical first-time home buyer in a particular area. NOT ones that sell multi-million dollar homes or work primarily on "listings", but rather within specific neighborhoods and price ranges.

I could just call them and say "Do you have anyone who needs to be pre-qualified for a loan?" But, then, what's in it for them? Look at them similar to the way we look at our other potential clients – determine what Personal Value you can bring to them and THEIR business. The better approach is to say "I've got some marketing ideas for you to get some new clients which can help both of us." So, I'll propose that we co-market to first-time home buyers, and share systems and resources for greater effect. How can we do this? Just for starters, we can co-host a first-time homebuyer seminar or teleconference call. We can offer free credit reports coupled with a consultation where I go over the report with the homebuyer. We can coordinate a budgeting session with a CPA to help them understand the home budgeting process, or provide a free one-hour consultation with an interior designer to help them with decorating ideas. Then, we can market these ideas to and through first-time homebuyers by using coordinated online and physical systems. Once the system is created, share the details with each team member.

Leaders know that the key to these external relationships is to approach them the same as they would their other customer relationships. Find out what your external agents need. Listen to their marketing ideas and business goals, and service them as you would a customer. This will build a relationship that will pay ongoing dividends for both you, your external partners, and your team members.

## 7. Rule of Risk

Les Brown has a quote that is a favorite of mine: "Jump first, and grow your wings on the way down!" If Gutenberg didn't take a chance on the printing press you might be reading this book as a manuscript handwritten by a monk! Another key trait of Leaders is that they are not afraid to take calculated risks. They experiment with new strategies, particularly in technology, and are not afraid to take that leap of faith. Studies show that there tend to be two types of people when it comes to making decisions. The first group evaluates information quickly, and acts decisively making a quick decision. This group is very slow to change their minds. The other group is just the opposite, taking a long time to make a decision, then after receiving information are quick to change their minds. Leaders fall into the first group. While they will not blindly make uninformed decisions, they understand the Rule of Risk, and are often willing to take a chance with a piece of technology a year or more before everyone else starts using it. Don't make rash decisions, but don't sit there and wait to see what "everyone else does" first. Embrace change and seek out cutting edge technologies that you think will give you a leg up on the competition. Then learn how to use these technologies creatively to enhance the customer experience and make your operation more effective.

Effective leaders know that their success is directly related to the success of their team members. Create an environment which nurtures and encourages personal and professional growth of individual team members. Keep communication a two-way street, and never stifle creativity or input from the team.

Weigh decisions carefully, but make a decision–and then stick with it. Remain open-minded, continually strive to learn new information about your industry, and expand your horizons at every turn.

Most importantly–respect and have fun with your team. They look up to you, and follow and effective leader faithfully on that "Road to Success!"

**Chip Tips:**

*Here are some "personal road signs" for you to take away from this Chapter:*

1. It's Not About <u>YOU!</u>

2. Leaders develop their relationships through Trust and Credibility.

3. Let the <u>CUSTOMER</u> make the decision – you need to narrow the focus of possible solutions.

4. Learn the 7 Rules of Success.

5. Leaders know how to work smarter – not harder, and aren't afraid to take calculated risks.

Cyrenius Forh, Jr.

Cyrenius Forh, Jr is a prolific writer, motivational speaker, successful entrepreneur and co-author of the book *Unleash The Winner Within You*. As founder and CEO of Life Empowerment Group International, Mr. Forh addresses three areas of empowerment—Spiritual Empowerment, Financial Empowerment, and Relational Empowerment. His talks and training sessions are thought provoking and motivating as he presents practical strategies for every aspect of intellectual, physical, social, emotional and spiritual development. Because of his high energy, he is known to all as *"Mr. Empowerment."* His life assignment is to inspire, empower and teach people *How To Live a Life of Influence and How To Move From The Life of The Ordinary to the Life of the Extraordinary*. Mr. Forh is a product of St. Agustine's College and Duke University Divinity School---both in North Carolina. As an ordained Minister of the Gospel, Mr. Forh is a man of strong faith and sound leadership. He's a loving husband and father who resides in Sacramento, California with his beautiful wife Edwina and their amazing children Vivian and Eurazmus.

**Life Empowerment Group International**
**P.O.Box 2814**
**Fairfield, California 94533**
**forhempowermentgroup@yahoo.com**
**or**
**www.theforhgroup.com**
**707-297-1653**

# The Spiritual Composition Of
# A Great Leader

"Before I formed you in the womb I knew you, before you were born I set you apart; I appointed you as a prophet to the nations." Then the LORD reached out his hand and touched my mouth and said to me, "Now, I have put my words in your mouth. See, today I appoint you over nations and kingdoms to uproot and tear down, to destroy and overthrow, to build and to plant." The word of the LORD came to me: "What do you see, Jeremiah?" "I see the branch of an almond tree," I replied. The LORD said to me, "You have seen correctly, for I am watching to see that my word is fulfilled." *—Jeremiah 1: 5,9-12 NKJV*

In his book *The 21 Irrefutable Laws of Leadership,* John C. Maxwell said, "The real leader holds the power, not just the position." That means he's equipped to do the job; he has the skills, gifts, talent and ability to guide, direct and instruct others to act for the best outcome.

Allow me to share with you some important characteristics of great leadership. Let me preface by declaring that every man and woman has leadership abilities. According to Genesis 1:26, God made man and give him, dominion and authority over the earth–charging him to be fruitful (produce), and to multiply (keep growing and increasing in life). It is ones divine destiny to operate in some leadership capacity. Be it in your home, at work, in your community or throughout the world…you have been given the right to lead. However, to be a leader is one thing, but a great leader is another level all together…and it's attainable. Simply put, great leadership starts within You.

During a church leadership conference last year, I was asked the question, "What does it take to become a *great leader*? And where do we begin when it comes to understanding our destiny as great leaders?" I responded that it begins with believing first, that you are a great leader, then, by envisioning yourself as a great leader. But to clearly understand your destiny as a great leader you must first understand *God's plan* for your life. He is the architect of *life,* the Creator of all things. He holds the blueprint to every soul – living or dead. He knows your gifts and your talents, your passion and your purpose. He placed in you everything you'll ever need to completely fulfill your destiny. He has given you dominion and authority in every aspects of life. And with specific assignments He has given set abilities. Therefore, in order to understand our position of authority, our leadership capacity and purpose, it is imperative that we seek God for the answer.

To be a leader in any capacity is no easy task. It is a great responsibility. It's life changing and challenging. It starts with you! You **must** start by leading yourself. If you wouldn't follow yourself why should anybody else? Train yourself to be great, by studying great leaders, knowing your passion, seeking God to discover your purpose on earth, by disciplining yourself to develop the right characteristics, and mental attitude. Becoming the person others want to follow will require honing certain skills, identifying your core values, fine-tuning your organizational and motivational skills. But here's the key: The secret to your success lies in your desire and willingness to *start.* Pat Summit, Head basketball coach of the Tennessee Lady Volunteers, once said, "Until you spread your wings, you'll have no idea how far you can fly."

As you ponder the attributes of great leaders, I present to you *The Spiritual Composition of A Great Leader* according to the book of Jeremiah, chapter one verses five, nine through twelve. Here you'll find five key attributes to being a great leader you can meditate on, translate and implement in your life as you endeavor to be the great leader you were created to be.

## I. A Great Leader Is Set Apart

*"Before I formed you in the womb I knew you, before you were born I set you apart..." —Jeremiah 1:5a*

A great leader has been called out from the rest of the leaders. You are a great leader. Why? Because God called you to be one among many. You were destined for greatness by the Lord before your were formed in your mothers womb. You are set apart according to the gifting of God and the authority He's ordained for your life. He has set you up for greatness. You are the creation of a great God. Pastor Cynthia Porter of Word of Faith Christian Center in Fairfield, California says, "You Are...Because He Is your Reality." Furthermore, being set apart validates the power of starting with "you"–in God. He's the great separator and elevator in life. He separates the doers from the slackers. He separates the haves from the have-nots. He separates the winners from the whiners. In short, starting with "you" in God sets you apart and places you in the winners' circle–a place that separates the successful people from the unsuccessful people.

According to God's plan for you, being set apart is to be one blessed to do great exploits. To be set apart as a leader, is to be sanctified, chosen, the elect to His holiness. In His eyes you have what it takes, no matter what you did in the past. However, you must believe in God first, then that you are a leader–diligent, faithful and willing to serve.

## II. A Great Leader Is Appointed

*"...I appointed you as a prophet to the nations." —Jeremiah 1:5b*

A great leader is appointed to do a set task. Most leaders know their appointments and are very much on top of them. They know to whom they have been assigned. Their role is to be committed to their assignment. A leader's appointment is his purpose in life...it is his passion (that which convicts him to act or change for the better) because he loves it. Now in the case of Jeremiah, because he did not know God's purpose for his life, there was no passion for being a prophet in the beginning. But God had to let him know that the reality of his making was to be a prophet to the nation. And when God appoints you there's nothing you can do or say to change it. For whatever you have been called to do, by God, He has qualified you, equipped you and sanctified you for the assignment. Therefore, it is safe to say that each one of us were created and appointed to fulfill a specific task here on earth for the glory of God.

### III.  Speaks Words of Power

*"Then the LORD reached out his hand and touched my mouth and said to me, "Now, I have put my words in your mouth." —Jeremiah 1:9*

A great leader is one who speaks power into the life of the people he leads. He speaks what he has been empowered to speak from God. His words reveal God's power of intention. That is, he speaks about what God intends to see take place in the lives of His people. The utterance of God is a spoken word implanted in the heart of the leader for an appointed time. The text says, *"Then the Lord reached out his hand and touched my mouth, and said now I have put my words in your mouth."* A great leader has been blessed to speak with wisdom. When he speaks people listen because it is life changing, empowering, motivating, educating, reproving with substance, and loving. You see, when God places His word in you, you become a "word carrying believer", and the word of God is life to the lifeless; it is light, or revelation, to the darkened mind and it is the manifestation of His love for people through Jesus Christ–the true Word. The word of God, given by God to a great leader fills his heart to overflowing, that when he speaks it comes out in abundance; abundance of power, love, wisdom, peace, joy, direction and prosperity. Therefore, if you desire to become a great leader ask God to fill your heart with His word, and to bless your mouth to speak His word for the betterment of the people you have been called to lead.

## IV. A Great Leader Has Vision:

*The word of the LORD came to me: "What do you see, Jeremiah?"*
*"I see the branch of an almond tree," I replied. The LORD said to me,*
*"You have seen correctly, for I am watching to see that my word is*
*fulfilled." —Jeremiah 1:11-12*

Great leaders have vision. They see *rightly* and understand what is *before* them. They are visionaries–they are called to take the vision given them to the nations, and to enlist them (the people) to participate in its realization. The Bible says, *"Where there is no vision, the people will perish."(Proverbs 29:18)*. He's the carrier of the vision to the people for their life. God told Jeremiah to look and tell Him what he saw. Jeremiah described what he saw and God said it was right. But the reality of this is that God rendered unto Jeremiah the vision. God never calls you to lead His people, or into leadership without a vision. The vision is for an appointed time in the lives of the people; that means your family, the company you work for, the organization you are heading or the team you captain or coach. If you are to lead in any of these capacity you must have a vision–or the people will perish. Theodore Hesburgh once said, *"The very essence of leadership is that you have to have a vision. The vision is the revelation of what is to come...it is the catalyst for the provision that it may manifest."* Habakkuk says, *"Write the vision, make it plain on tablets that he who sees it shall run with it."* A great leader empowers his people by helping them see, understand and feel the purpose of the vision. Thus, they run with it and are blessed. The vision of a leader is for the ones who follow him. W.A. Nance once said, *"No person can be a great leader unless he takes genuine joy in the success of those under him. He must see the joy it will bring God and the people who par-take of the fulfillment of the vision."*

## V. A Great Leader Advocates Change

*See, today I appoint you over nations and kingdoms to uproot and tear down, to destroy and overthrow, to build and to plant." —Jeremiah 1:10*

A great leader advocates change. He believes that change is good for the growth and advancement of the people. He believes that change brings about transformation, which begins with perception.

**Romans12:2b** says, *"Be ye transformed by the renewing of your mind."* That means having a mind's eye for change will bring to fruition change. Simply put, in order to have positive change transpire in your life you must first see yourself in that change.

The great Les Brown once said, *"You must keep yearning, learning and earning."* How you see yourself changing depends on how you feed your mind with what or where you want to be. A great leader believes that in order for you to become someone you've never been, or to achieve something you've never achieved, you must begin to do the things you've never done—beginning with renewing your mind. If you have always had a poor man's mentality you will always find it hard to understand the principles of prosperity. You will always talk about being rich one day...but never achieving it. Why? Because it's only a desire for you; a dream that you do not yet believe...For no man, or woman, can climb beyond the limitations of their own belief.

The question, however, is what are you doing to change your mindset so that your desires become realities in your life? Gandhi once said, *"Be the change you want to see in your world."* My father once said, "Change begins with a thought." Start by thinking rich. See yourself successful. The Bible says, *"As a man thinketh so is he."* In other words, you are who you think you are. Also, you must speak what you believe you are. To do that you must first fill your heart with positive energy, affirming that you are successful by speaking success into your life.
Read about and study successful people. Learn more than just who they are; know how they live and know their strategies for successful living. Apply what you've learned. Ask them for help—get mentored. Fill your life with what you desire to become and speak it into reality. The Bible says, *"Out of the abundance of the heart, the mouth will speak."* Thus, we can change our situation, our lives and our position by first changing our mindset, which changes our view point of life, which changes our heart, which will reveal the evidence of change when we speak—for those things that be not, becomes reality with our spoken word...which will create a change in our surroundings.

## Final Thought

I challenge you to see yourself as the great leader that you are. To dare to be separate, set apart from the slothful generalities of life and to be fixed, and focused on your divine destiny; to be a visionary, always seeing yourself as God sees you–victorious, prosperous and wise; to know you're assigned to greatness for such a time as this; to be one who speaks power into the lives of those you lead, as well as those you meet. And to always be prepared to embrace change. Remember, it all starts with *YOU.*

Dave Sheffield

Dave Sheffield has touched the lives of thousands of people with his electrifying message. From students to CEO's, Dave Sheffield brings boundless energy and connection to his presentations. His topics focus on the fundamental characteristics of leadership. Whether it is in leading a family, or a multi-billion dollar company; Dave Sheffield's message not only connects with the audience, but drives them to immediate action!

Dave started his first company at the age of 19. By applying the lessons he teaches in his 11 Commandments of Leadership programs, he built solid, strong sales forces. His clients include: Monster.com, Clear Channel Radio, Nikken Health Systems, Jaycees International, Valley Shelter Homes, Electrolux, and Saladmaster.

**He can be reached at:**
David Sheffield
6 Hillcrest Ct.
Eldridge, IA 52748

(563) 285-6191
1-800-863-2591

www.theshef.com

# The 11 Commandments of Leadership

Have you ever wondered what made some people stand out in a crowd? These people are not people that just blend in, they are people that others want to follow, to be like. What if you could be one of those people? How would your life be different?

During this short time together, I'm going to share with you some of the things that I have learned by studying some of the world's greatest leaders. Some of the people mentioned you may have heard of, others you wouldn't recognize. Just the same, these people have made their mark on the world, have led and empowered, and have even had numerous critics. But they have all possessed eleven qualities that you are about to read of. So grab you highlighter, because The Shef is going to help take you to another level!

## The 11 Commandments of Leadership

1.  **Integrity**
2.  **Vision**
3.  **Be flexible**
4.  **Delegate and empower**
5.  **Tune in to other people's needs**
6.  **Public praise, private critique**
7.  **Look at the competition**
8.  **Build yourself**
9.  **Know to say no**
10. **Give Back**
11. **Association**

## Integrity

When I was a young man, my dad was shopping for a car. After numerous trips to car lots, he found a great car. It looked great, and the salesman was making an unbeatable offer! My dad didn't take the offer. After we left, I asked him how he could have passed up such an unbelievable offer. He simply told me that he didn't trust the man who was trying to sell it to him. "You can't get a great deal from a not so great guy."

There is no such thing as situational ethics. Look at the ethics scandals that rocked the world in the early 2000s. Fortunes were lost, people went to prison, and dreams were dashed. All because of a lack of integrity.

## Vision

Success is not an accident. If you are with a company, own a business, are in a relationship, or are on a team, you've bought into someone's vision. Every successful person I have met has one common thread: They keep and maintain written goals. Life does not happen by accident, but yet most of us put more thought into what we are making for dinner than how we want to create abundance in our lives.

Yale University did a study of their 1953 graduating class. They interviewed each graduate and asked them two questions. Do you keep and maintain written goals? Do you have a plan to achieve these goals? Only 3% of the respondents answered yes!

After 20 years, they interviewed the surviving members of the class and found that those 3% that had written goals were worth more in financial terms than the other 97% combined!

My challenge to you is that before you lay your head on your pillow this evening, you dream a little. WRITE DOWN YOUR DREAMS, AND GIVE THEM A DEADLINE! Even the faintest ink on a napkin is more powerful than the best laid out plan in your head.

Living life without goals is like going into the woods with a shotgun, firing off 5 rounds, and hoping that something good will run into it. Something magic happens when you put pen to paper. Vision also

keeps us real. Don't ever trade what you want right now for v
want most in life.

## Be Flexible

Leaders are rigid in their principals, but flexible in their approach. Great leaders are not afraid to try new things. They are also not afraid to stop doing things that are not working. After all, insanity is defined as doing the same thing over and over again, but expecting a different result. Think of a fly banging against the screen of a window, trying to get to the free world outside. Freedom may only be a few feet or even inches away, but they will keep trying the old way until they dic. Sound familiar?

## Delagate and Epower

Henry Ford was sitting before a senate inquiry and was getting badgered. Most of the senators were upset that he was trying to bankrupt the buggy whip industry. Henry was not an educated man, but he surrounded himself with experts. One particularly belligerent senator began asking Mr. Ford about the inner properties of the internal combustion engine. When he faltered, the senator exclaimed, "You claim to have this great invention that will help this country, but you can't even tell us how it works!" At that moment, Henry Ford had enough. He shot out of his chair and rebuked, "I don't clutter my head with every miniscule detail. While I may not know all of the answers personally, I can summon a room full of experts on any subject you may want at the snap of a finger!" The questioning stopped.

What are some things that you are doing right now that could be done by others? How could you not only delegate that task to them, but also make them feel part of the team? Answering these 2 questions will catapult your business and life to new heights!

## Tune into Other People's Needs

OK, quiz time. God gave you how many ears (two) how many mouths (one) USE THEM ACCORDINGLY!!!. Zig Ziglar reminds us that, "You can get anything you want by helping enough other people get what they want." Everyone is constantly listening to his or her favorite radio station, WIIFM, or What's in it for ME?

One of my mentors and best friends, Joe Delvecchio is a genius at helping others realize what they want, and he helps them get there. When we had a contest in our direct sales business that would pay Joe an extra $30,000 bonus if we hit target that month, Joe came up with a plan. I'll never forget the phone call at 7:00 am on a Sunday morning. On the other end of the line was Joe saying, "Dave, you will make enough money this month to buy a house! You will make more than $20,000 this month!" That woke me up. I began to come up with a plan to make it happen. The result: I made over $20,000 in 3 weeks, and Joe got his bonus. Even though I was 22 years old, I realized that the best part was because of the programs, and the dream outlines that we helped create for every person working with us, not only did they make great money; they realized that they could grow into a new zone of lifestyle! I still use that same method of success mapping in my live programs.

## Public Praise, Private Critique

If you want screaming, go to a hockey game. The workplace is not a place for you to parade the mistake of a team member in front of everyone in the office. Most of the time people are far harder on themselves than you ever would have been. I have found one of the most effective ways of correcting workplace challenges is to have the person come into my office, sit in my chair, and ask him what he would say about the situation if he were in my shoes. This does 2 things. 1. It trains them to think like a leader. 2. It helps you get to the root of the thought process that created the problem in the first place.

Conversely, when someone does something right- PRAISE! Public, loud, and often. They may tell you that they're embarrassed you're doing it, but they love it! I have gotten far more mileage out of a pat on the back than anything I could have bought for a contest.

## Look at the Competition

If you think that you have a niche in the market with your business, and no one will compete with you, you're wrong. The competition can help you see what may be working, and also what is not!

One of the greatest illustrations of this is the Von Maur Corporation.

They are a family owned high-end department store chain with 25 or so stores in the Midwest. When people started looking to discount retailers, many higher end stores cut their prices to try and compete with the Wal-Mart, Target, and Shopko type of stores. Did Von Maur cut prices, NO! They made the guests feel more at home. They added so much value to the services they offered their guests, that they were willing to invest in the shopping experience. Not only that, they offered a charge card at 0% interest that people could make monthly payments on. I would highly suggest visiting one of the Von Maur stores. You will notice an impeccably decorated and designed store. Turn a corner and enjoy a piano player playing some of your favorite songs.

Does this sound crazy? When other stores were going belly up, Von Maur was growing. The charge card also allowed many customers to rationalize the ability to spend more without the guilt adding to the Visa bill. The result: 50% of VonMaur's sales are on the charge card, and the sales are booming. I am proud to call the President of the company, Jim Von Maur, a good friend. Whenever we discuss business, it is clear to me that the company will continue to dominate the market!

### Build Yourself

Imagine you are walking into a beautiful mansion. The people who live there are extremely successful in every facet of life. You walk thru the front door and look to the left and right. What room is there? A den with volumes of books.

Do you think that the people said, "Some day we will be very rich and will build a room that will force us to buy a ton of books, just to fill the shelves. Barnes and Noble will love us!" I doubt that very highly. Any person whom I have met that is considered "successful" realizes that reading is like telling life that you are serious about using all of your abilities and life will reward you. Go to seminars, listen to audio books. If you can't afford to, you need to. The library is an excellent resource for many foundations for your dream's building blocks!

Jim Rohn, who is one of the most sought after speakers in the world, says that you could forget to eat for a day, but never forget to read!

### Know to say "No"

Time is the one equal in life. Also, no one has your best interest in mind like you do. How many times have you felt overwhelmed, going thru your days only to find that you are simply pleasing other's demands? Discover the joy of "No"

Worried if you'll offend someone? If you only knew how often other people thought of you, you'd stop caring what they thought of you.

### Give Back

There are so many ways you can give back. Some are financial, some are just involving your time. I fully believe that giving starts the receiving process. I don't care what you do to give thanks. There is something magical when you brighten a person's day by just volunteering. Get involved with the community or your favorite charity.

God's gift to you was your life. Your gift back to him is what you do with it. If you don't think you have the means or the talent, call me. I guarantee I can share stories of people that have done far more with far less.

### Association

Successful people only surround themselves with the best quality of people. Les Brown says that your income will be the average of the 5 people you spend the most time with. The same is true for other areas of life. Stretch yourself, bump that comfort zone, surround yourself with those who demand more of you than you think you can give, and reap some of these great rewards that life has to offer you!

A constant trait in those who are the best of the best is that they surround themselves with the best. Not just people who are good, but those whom are truly gifted, and yes even better than them. This is not only in a professional field, but it is true in life as well. If your son or daughter was 13 and started to run with the "rough crowd" would you want them to pick better friends? And why? That's right! If you want to see who you will be in 5 years, simply look at the 5 people you spend the most time with.

The fact that you have made the investment in this book tells me that you are a winner in the game of life. Life is not a spectator sport. I am honored that you have decided to invest the time with me in this book, and hope to either talk to you on my audio programs, or even at your youth, college, or business event. Until next time! Enjoy the journey of your life! THE SHEF

Dawn Strozier

Dawn Strozier is a Certified Personal Trainer and Nutrition Consultant who enjoys sharing with people a high energy message on how to be fit for life and live up to your fullest potential. It is a message she has learned from her own life.

Dawn was born in Cleveland Ohio where she discovered her passion to succeed, while pursuing a dancing career. That pursuit of dance took her to Los Angeles, California where she quickly learned it will not only take talent and hard work, but a transitional mind-set to obtain success. A mind-set, which she travels the country sharing with audiences everywhere.

She has conducted hundreds of trainings, seminars, and women's empowerment symposiums for companies such as Level 10 International, ACN Network, Elite Marketing and Clear Net Corporations just to name a few. Some of her subjects include health & wellness, leadership, motivation, and overcoming obsticles. With her dynamic speaking style and her passion for people, Dawn's customized presentations will teach, inspire, and channel audiences to new levels of achievement.

**Dawn Strozier**
369 S. Doheny Dr.
Beverly Hills, CA 90211

(310) 535-9577
dawn@dawnspeaks.com

# Mastering The Keys To Effective Leadership

Get ready to transform yourself for success. Mastering these keys to effective leadership will help you tackle the inner work needed to Unleash the Leader Within You.

John C. Maxwell in the "21 Indispensable Qualities of A Leader" states – Everything rises and falls with leadership. I believe success is within reach for everyone, but success will not come without leadership. Leadership ability determines a persons' level of effectiveness and you cannot produce consistently on a level higher then your leadership.

In order for you to reach the highest of heights, to live up to your fullest potential, and to achieve great success you must master these keys:

**The 1st Key**

<u>V</u>ision – *It's everything to a leader*

> *"If you have but one wish let it be for an idea"*
> **—Robert Johnson**

Robert Johnson launched the first cable network aimed at African American audiences, created the first African American controlled company on the New York stock exchange, and built BET into the nations largest minority cable network. He later sold his flagship cable company and most of his other media properties to Viacom for $3 Billion, making him, in 2001, the richest African American in the United States.

By his own admission Robert Johnson entered into the cable TV business through total serendipity, after getting a job at the Cable Trade Association, because a young lady he just met told him he would make a good lobbyist. Johnson started hobnobbing with businessmen who began to orientate him into the cable world.

Once Johnson understood technology and saw that it could take a signal and send it all across the country simultaneously to different stations, then it became clear to him that programming could be segmented and targeted to different audiences.

Armed with just a $15,000 bank loan, a business plan and a strong vision of what he wanted to accomplish, Johnson began to go after his dreams. His big break came when cable magnate John Malone, CEO of Tele-Communication Inc., the countries third largest cable company, decided to invest in his company. In spite of the fact Johnson had no prior knowledge of running a business and the only real entrepreneurial experience he possessed was a paper route growing up, Malone could see Johnson would work harder for himself then anyone else and bought into his vision.

Although faced constant struggle to get the cable operator to value the black households in their neighborhood the same way they valued the white households, being told by advertisers "We don't need to reach the black consumers," and told by critics his programming could be better. Johnson, going mostly by his gut, continued to compete against the odds and ultimately built BET holding into the largest minority cable channel in the country reaching 55 million U.S. households.

## Tying it all together

Effective leaders have a vision of what they want to accomplish, and that vision becomes the driving force that pushes through all obstacles.

Vision comes before the ability to lead. However, people don't follow the vision itself, they follow the leader who has the ability to effectively communicate that vision.

When you have a clear focus on where you want to go, you will begin to attract the very resources you need.

Vision is everything to a leader. You show me a leader without a vision and I'll show you a leader parked on the side of the road.

## The 2nd Key

**Influence** – *The true meaning of leadership*

> *You achieve excellence as a leader, when people will follow you everywhere. Even if it's only out of curiosity*
> ### — Collin Powel

Influence is who you are and how you, as a person, impact the message you carry.

Influence magnifies your leadership abilities, improves your parenting skills, affects your relationships and helps you sell yourself as a person. The very essence of influence is getting people to participate.

People will not follow someone they do not trust and whose character they believe is flawed. To increase your influence you must first look at your character.

## Tying it all together

Ask yourself whether your words and actions match all the time. When you say your going to do something, do you always follow through? When you tell your children you're going to take them here or that you will show up at their recital, do you do it? Can people trust your handshake?

Examine the answers to these questions. Understand that the respect a leader needs to have influence requires that ones ethics be without question.

Identify your areas of weakness and create a plan that will prevent you from making the same mistakes again.

## The 3rd Key

## <u>S</u>elf Discipline – *Paying the price for what you want*

*Foolish people want to conquer the world, wise people*
*first make it a point to conquer themselves*
### — *Author Unknown*

The first person you lead is you. Leaders can never take others farther then they have gone themselves.

Discipline is the ability to make yourself do the things you have to do when they need to be done, regardless of how you feel.

Of all the leaders this nation has ever seen Theodore Roosevelt was one of the toughest mentally and physically. But he did not start that way. As a child he was very sickly. He had a debilitating asthma, poor eyesight, and was very frail. Doctors weren't sure he would survive.

At twelve years of age, Roosevelt's father told him "you have the mind but you don't have the body and without the help of the body you can not go far. You must develop the body," and develop the body he did.

Through Discipline and hard work Roosevelt spent time every day, building his body and his mind. He worked hard ice-skating, boxing, weight lifting, and reading literature of people he admired. By the time he graduated from Harvard Roosevelt was ready to conquer the world, and in 1909 he became the President of the United States.

On January 6, 1919, at his home in New York, Roosevelt died in his sleep. After hearing the news, Vice President Marshall said "Death had to take him in his sleep for if Roosevelt had been awake, there would have been a fight." When they removed him from his bed they found a book under his pillow. Theodore Roosevelt was still striving to learn and improve up to the very last minute. A discipline he developed as a child.

## Tying it all together

*Making discipline a life style:*
- Identify your priorities
- Stay focused on your results
- Eliminate excuses
- Go after it as if your life depended on it

> *Remember only in the moment of discipline*
> *do you have power to achieve your dreams.*
> ### *— John C. Maxwell*

## The 4th Key

**Inspiration** – *The highest calling of a leader*

> *Look at a man as he is and he only becomes worse.*
> *But if you look at a man as he could be*
> *then he becomes what he should be.*
> ### *—Author Unknown*

The growth and development of people is the highest calling of leadership. Sam Walton said, "Outstanding leaders go out of their way to boost the self esteem of their personnel, and when people believe in themselves it's amazing what they can accomplish."

Leaders know how to bring out the best in people. They know that the deepest principle in human nature is the craving to be important.

History sparkles with amusing examples of famous people struggling for a feeling of importance. George Washington wanted to be called "His Mightiest, the President of the United States." Columbus pleaded for the title "Admiral of the Ocean and Viceroy of India." Catherine the Great refused to open letters that were not address to "Her Imperial Majesty," and Mr. Lincoln in the white house turned upon Mr. Grant like a tigress and shouted, "How dare you be seated in my presence until I invite you." One of the best things you can do for a person is believe in them. People don't care how much you know until they know how much you care. And once they realize how much you truly care about them and their desires they are yours. You will have loyal followers who are willing to develop and grow.

## Tying it all together

In order to become an effective leader you most appreciate the value of people. Make sure every member of your team has the opportunity to make meaningful and lasting contributions.

Look for gifts, talents and uniqueness in others then help them increase for their benefit and the benefit of the entire team. It is your responsibility as a leader to inspire and encourage people to realize their fullest potential.

Inspiration and empowerment is oxygen to the soul.

## The 5th Key

**Organization** – *A must for every leader*

It's not how hard you work its how smart you work. The ability to juggle several different projects successfully is a must for every leader. However, the key to effectiveness is to think and do the things in order of priority.

In effective organization you must determine what 20 percent of the work will give you 80 percent of the return and focus your energy, time, and resources there. This is commonly known as the 20/80 principle.

Delegating responsibility is another important factor in organization. Not only does delegating less important work allow you to focus on things that are a priority, but it also creates a sense of signifigance in others.

## Tying it all together

A secure leader is not afraid to give up responsibility. A leader realizes it makes them more effective and it empowers their team.

Delegate, delegate, delegate.

**The 6th Key**

**Never stop bettering your best** – *To keep leading, keep learning.*

> *It's what you learn after you know everything that counts.*
> **—John Wooden, Hall of Fame basketball coach**

In todays world improvement is necessary just to keep up with the changes that are taking place rapidly. People who have more information have a tremendous advantage over people who don't. Though it may take years to acquire the knowledge needed to become super successful, simple behaviors can make a substantial difference in your level of success and give you an edge that others simply don't have.

## Tying it all together

**Bettering Your Best**

- Reading for an hour each day – consider a speed reading course
- Studying the lives of great people – biography and audio-biographies
- Turn television time into learning time – watch biography or A&E television network
- Attend conferences and retreats
- Hire a personal coach
- Commit to life long learning

## Conclusion:

I want to encourage you to review this chapter periodically to measure how you are developing as a leader. The "Tying It All Together" section of this chapter was designed to help you master each quality and start you on the process of continuous personal growth.

Leadership starts from the inside out, and I believe after "Mastering These Keys to Effective Leadership," success is yours. There will be nothing you can't accomplish.

Greg Cook

Greg Cook started his journey for personal development in the United States Marine Corps. Growing up in an inner city area he learned the phrase "if it is to be it is up to me" very early in life. Greg Cook graduated with honors in finance using benefits from the Marines to help pay for his college. He delivers speeches, workshops and trainings to a vast majority of sales and financial professionals. He has served on boards and committees of local companies and organizations.

Greg Cook believes in the givers gain philosophy. What you give is what you get.

He currently works with companies in a consultant capacity having developed strategies to help build sales organizations and management teams.

Greg Cook bought his first piece of real estate at the age of 20. He started his first company at the age of 21 that was a financial company offering mortgages, insurance and investments. He has since bought, sold and financed millions of dollars of real estate.

Greg Cook has spent an enormous amount of time learning the power of the mind and even has developed personal power and positive mind power workshops for making life long positive changes.

Greg Cook travels from Detroit, Michigan
(419) 480-8180 Office
**www.GregCook.com**, **greg@GregCook.com** or **PersonalTalk@aol.com**

# Semper Fi leadership...
# business style!

Semper Fi. Some of the readers may have heard this before. Semper Fi is short for Semper Fidelis which is the motto of the United States Marine Corps. Semper Fidelis is latin for "always faithful." Always faithful to God, country, family and the Corps. It kind of reminds me of a saying that Vince Lombardi had, which was God, family and the Green Bay Packers. I like Vince Lombardi as a person from the past to look at for leadership traits. (I am not a Packers fan even though my son is...Go Lions!) To begin, obviously I am a former Marine. Some may say that leaders are born; however, maybe some are but I firmly believe that the majority of the leaders that are out there are made.

Leadership is a very important quality or characteristic for you to have. If you are going to try and build a company, division, department or small business you should spend some time on learning about leadership. Obviously you're reading this book so you are interested in learning about leadership. When you look at 2 organizations who are matched up against each other whether it is a sports game, business competition or even a military battle you can have both organizations being equal in size, strength and resources; however, with all things being equal the difference in which team will be the victor goes to the team with the better leader.

So, how are leaders made? Well, I think some are self made. Through self help books, tapes, workshops, conferences and anything else you can get your hands on to grow. That's right to grow. Grow as a person in wisdom, knowledge and understanding. In your self as well as in others and even the human mind if you go that far.

To grow in your self is to become more. You can never "get" more until you become more. Whatever your "get" is. Whether or not it is family, money, houses, cars or even prestige. Motivational speaker Les Brown once said you don't get in life what you want, you get in life what you are.

Jim Rohn who is a multi-millionaire and very wise, is someone I have been a student of for a long time has a saying that "if you work on your job you can make a living, but if you work on your self you can make a fortune."

I do whole speeches and conferences around leadership. I only have so much space in this book so I want to try and really give you the meat and potatoes. I can't give you every possible thing I have to give on leadership; however, I truly feel that after this chapter you will have a strong foundation along with the other chapters to really be on your way to becoming a better leader and "Unleash the Leader Within You."

There are many many traits that can be attributed to leadership. I am not even going to try and name or describe them all. But I am going to go over some important points. The first is confidence. Or some may refer to as self confidence. There are many people out there that have once lacked self confidence only to later in life gain it. Self-Confidence is something that you see in a leader. However, most leaders were not always confident in themselves. Fortunately self-confidence is something that you can learn. It's called practice. When you do something good over and over you reinforce in your self that you "can do it."

Arnold Schwarzenegger said "I don't listen to those who say I can't."

Gaining self confidence. Some easy ways to do this is to first face the things that you fear. Whatever it may be. Some people are afraid to make cold calls to prospects. Some people are afraid to "ask for the sale." Even some others are afraid to get their clients to "write a check." Still others are afraid of confrontation. Whatever you may not feel strong with THAT is what you need to work on to grow as a person and as a leader. Leaders face their problems. Leaders make a personal inventory of their strengths and weaknesses. They then capitalize on their strengths and then try to minimize on their weaknesses. By minimizing I mean to face them and then conquer them. Also, if you at least face them and then realize you just don't like doing that task. You can find ways around it, such as you are a business owner and you dread getting on the phone to make cold calls. You absolutely must face it. After you have looked directly at your fear and dealt with it you can continue to get better at doing it. Repetition, doing something over and over again is the only way to get good at anything. Just ask any pro athlete. Once you have overcame your fear you can do it again, again and again. The Marine in me says anything that doesn't kill you will make you stronger. Now, you can build your business or career up to a point that maybe you then employ someone to do that task to free up your time to doing the things that you like to do.

I do some corporate consulting. However, with my practice that I have built up I do speaking engagements on different topics a few are: sales, marketing, leadership, achievement, personal power and overcoming adversity. I have talked on other topics but I think you get the idea. Where I am going with this is that when I was younger I feared giving an oral book report or presentation to the class while I was in school. As a matter of fact I can remember how I thought I might as well die when I was to give an oral report and remember talking my mother to go out to breakfast after an early morning dentist appointment just to miss that class. I bring that up because after I faced my fears later in life I did more and more public talks where today I feel very comfortable talking to people. As a matter of fact I love talking to people.

I recently heard Donald Trump say on his TV show *The Apprentice* that if you are going to be a success in anything you have to have passion. My passion is to help people. Whether that help is in their personal or professional lives. Nothing makes me feel better than when I receive a letter, card, email, voice mail or even personal phone calls on how I was able to positively make an impact on a persons life for the better.

In one of my businesses I have employed people in different capacities. I once had a manager who was very knowledgeable in his field. However, he just wasn't a people person. As a manager or leader you really have to be able to work with people. And, if you are in a profession that deals with customers or clients then you really need to be a people person. There is an old saying that you can attract more bees with honey than you can with vinegar. Well that is true with people too. A manager I once had clearly spelled out his management style which was it was going to be his way or the highway. One time while sitting down with another person in the office he asked "What's your problem?" That person proceeded to tell him exactly what they thought of him. And, it wasn't pretty. If they don't like it…fire them he said. Well, if you work with people like that you better hire a good Human Resource department because you will be going through employees. A lot of employees. That style was in the past; however, there is no place for that type of my way or the highway in today's marketplace. The people you will be or are leading want to feel important. "What can I do for you?" is a common statement of a business owner I know in Ohio. Remember people do not care how much you know until they know how much you care. Now listen to the two different ways of talking to people, first "What is your problem?" and then secondly "What can I do for you?" The first one is almost feeling as if the person doesn't even like you whereas the second one you can most definitely feel like you matter. So, if they have an issue let them talk. It may help you understand where they are coming from and maybe even let you know how others perceive you as a leader. And, hopefully you like what you hear.

Leaders understand being of service to their customers. Both their external clients their customers and their internal clients their employees. The best leaders serve. Most leaders understand doing more than what their paid for. How many times people out there have said something like it's not my job. If you always do what you've always done you'll always get what you always got. So, you have to do more. I like the following story about doing more and being of service: One night many years ago an older man and his wife came into a hotel trying to get out of the rain. The couple approached the front desk hoping to get some shelter for the night. "Could you possibly give us a room here" the husband asked the front clerk. The clerk was a friendly man and smiled to the couple but explained to the couple that there were 3 conventions in town and every room is booked up the clerk said. But I can't send a nice couple like you out into the rain at One O'clock in the morning he explained. Would you folks perhaps be interested in sleeping in my room for the night. "It's not much and definitely not a suite but it would give you a place to stay and make you folks comfortable for the night" the clerk said. And, when the couple declined the young man pressed on he said to them, "don't worry about me I'll make out just fine." So, the couple agreed to take the young mans room for the night. The next morning when the older couple was checking out, the elderly man said to the clerk you are the kind of manager that should be the boss of the best hotel in the United States. Maybe one day I will build one for you to run. The elderly couple and the clerk looked at each other, smiled and had a good laugh. As the older couple left they talked and agreed that the helpful clerk was indeed exceptional as finding a friendly and helpful person was not that easy. Later. As almost 2 years had passed, the clerk had almost even forgotten the incident with this couple and the cold stormy night, when the older couple had summonsed the young man through a letter recalling the night he had helped them and enclosed a round trip ticket asking him to come and visit with them in New York. The old man met him there in New York at the corner of 5th Avenue and 34th Street he then pointed up to a great new building that looked like a palace. That there said the old man is the new hotel I have just built for you to run. You must be joking the young man said. I can assure you that I am not joking the older man said. The older mans name was William Waldorf Astor. The magnificent structure was the original Waldorf Astoria Hotel. And, the young clerk who became the first manager of the Waldorf Astoria Hotel was George C. Boldt who gave up his room so the older couple could have a good nights rest. The story may be a bit embellished as some are; however, the basic facts here about this story is true. Isn't that a great servant hood story. You just never know how acts of kindness and being of service come back to you. I guess the question after that story is what do you think you would've done in that situation? I think many of us can learn from the extraordinary service given from George C. Boldt. Leaders are extraordinary. They are ordinary with something extra. So many people think that leaders are super and that they are just so much more when in reality they just a little extra. And that is how you too can become a leader by just doing that something extra.

The American Dream of financial freedom is alive and doing well. And, I am a living testimony to it. In some of my workshops I have written the word "AMERICAN" down on the board and underlined the last four letters. The last four letters in the word American is "ican." Whatever it is in life you want to do, the first step is just saying "I can do it." I even go so far as to tell the audience to point at themselves with their finger tapping themselves with their pointed finger while making it personal to them when they are saying "I can do it." Repeat after me. "I can do it!" Say it, "I can do it!" Pointing to yourself saying "I can do it!" The Marine in me is now coming out. Louder. "I can do it!" now, like you mean it "I can do it!." Yes you can. Henry Ford once said "whether you think you can or think you can't...you're right."

I am going to leave you with one last quote.

> *"Man who says it can not be done*
> *should not interrupt he who is doing it."*
> — ***Chinese Proverb***

Hassan Omar

Hassan Omar is an author, coach, speaker, and business professional with more than 17 years of experience in financial services management, strategic planning, training, and change management.

He is the founder and CEO of the Atlanta-based Vertical Passing Enterprises; and is the current Director of Community Affairs for the Atlanta Chapter of The National Black MBA Association; the largest chapter of the largest professional association of African Americans in the United States.

The pillars of his success are ten years of leadership service in the U.S. Army, and the wealth of experience gained from supporting a range of private and fortune 100 companies. He has personally trained thousands of individuals around the world; using his experience to help them to discover the tools that are within to meet and exceed their personal and professional goals.

Want to know more about Hassan?

He can be reached via **www.verticalpassing.com**.

Email: **hassan.omar@verticalpassing.com**

**678-643-7556**

# Lead Yourself, & The Rest Will Follow

This chapter is more than just a collection of thoughts and ideas. It's my way of sharing the experiences that led me to where I am today, and the answers I found when I asked:

*How am I supposed to lead others, when I can barely lead myself?*

## The Challenge of Leadership

> *Leadership is the art of getting someone else to do something you want ... because he wants to do it.*
>
> **–General Dwight D. Eisenhower**

Leadership is easy…when you have passion and a plan. Easy when your desire to succeed is so intense that it inspires others to embrace your dreams as if they were their own. Easy, when you have a system to achieve it. And even easier when someone has done this for you.

As a Sergeant in the U.S. Army, one of the easier things I had to do was lead for others. Given a mission, some men, and a map, it was done. I'd love to be able to attribute that success to my charisma, skill, or strength of will; but it wouldn't be the truth.

The truth is that I succeeded because the hard part, turning a vision into a plan, was already done for me. By following my superiors' plans, there was no doubt that I was going to succeed; all I had to do was act.

---

I realized this when trying to act on my own. The success that I had achieved for others didn't happen when I tried to do the same for myself. Gone was the confidence, will, and ease in which things got done; in was procrastination, fear of failure, and self-doubt.

The challenge I faced then, was the same one that many struggle with today; motivating myself to accomplish things that were important to me, just because I wanted to; to lead myself.

I answered it with vision and passion.

**Inspiration, Meet Opportunity**

> *The Essence of Leadership is Vision...*
> *It is the capacity to transform an idea from dream to reality.*
> **—Unknown**

In a nutshell, your vision is what you want to do. It is the purpose behind all you do, and that "thing" that inspires you. It can be as simple as painting a room, or as complex as a work of art. Either way, it's your idea, its' important, and its' what you're going to do.

Of course to achieve it, you've got to see it…

Most of us have some pretty good ideas in our heads. We'd love to act on them, but for some reason can't. Maybe the time or money isn't right, or maybe we just need to see, as Paul Harvey says, *"the rest of the picture."*

Prior to writing this, I had a long-held desire to write and share my thoughts. I had plenty of ideas and lots to say, but not a clue as how I'd do it.

All of the pieces fell into place when the opportunity to co-write this book appeared.

It happened late one evening as I was just about ready to hang up on a conference call. For some reason, I paused. Good thing I did, because

Kevin Bracy was about to lay it out. As he did, everything came together, and there it was – *the rest of the picture!*

...and once you see it, you've got to believe it.

## Make your vision your passion

Outside of God, family, and Country, it has to be the most important thing in the world to you. It's your idea; not your family's, not your friends', and until they buy into it, certainly not the people that'll help you achieve it.

Charm and charisma only goes so far, eventually you'll have to show what you know. This is accomplished by learning everything there is to know about your goal and what it takes to reach it. That means research, research, and a side dish of research! Success comes with hours of reading, networking, and training. Yes, it's a lot of work; but in the end, you'll see it's worth it.

The more you know, the more it shows. The more it shows, the more your passion flows. The more your passion flows, the quicker everyone's confidence and interest in your idea will grow; and that's half the fight.

But of course a vision is but a dream, and passion is just a load of hot air if it doesn't become reality; so you have to make a plan.

## Make Dreams Reality

Believe it or not, this is the easy part. Your vision articulates what you're going to do, your passion inspires you, and your plan simply states how you're going to do it.

The military provides some of the best tools available to ensure its' leaders success. One tool, lets' call it the **L.E.A.D.E.R.** system, is a reliable approach to problem solving. By helping the user break down problems into a series of logical steps, complex problems can be solved more efficiently, and leaders can be more effective.

The **L.E.A.D.E.R.** system:

**L**isten to your Heart
**E**xamine your goal
**A**ct decisively
**D**evelop the plan
**E**xecute
**R**eward yourself

If you are struggling with an issue that's challenging you, I strongly recommend that you use the system. I've used many times to tackle challenges in life. For example:

After nearly a decade of distinguished military service, I reached the point where I felt that I had done enough, and wanted a 'normal' life. But walking away and starting over wouldn't be easy; I needed a plan.

The Army is not just a job; it's a way of life. I went to places that most people don't, and did things that most won't. It was interesting way of life, and I liked it, and after a few years, couldn't imagine life any other way.

That picture was shattered when a new supervisor was assigned to me. To say our personalities clashed would be a gross understatement; it was worse. I hated him, and he couldn't stand me. Unfortunately, he out-ranked me, and could do anything within his power to undermine me; he did it well. Suddenly, everything I did was wrong. No longer considered a "rising star," now I was "lazy, irresponsible, and not trust worthy." In a culture where image really matters, those words from my superior became the "kiss of death" for my career.

Seeing how I was stuck with this individual, and knowing that I was probably going to lose the fight, I seriously began thinking about leaving. But where could my family and I go, and what would we do? Leaving the service would force us to completely start over, and we'd be all alone. How could I convince the Missus to trust me on this, and believe that we could make it on our own?

By **L**istening to my heart.

What was my heart telling me? That it was time to go, and that we could make it.

But what else could I be doing? And how were we going to do it?

I didn't have the answers; so I had to look deeper.

## Examining and understanding your goal

There are many benefits that come with serving your country; but personal freedom isn't one of them! I wanted to be free. But regaining it would mean sacrificing lifestyle we were accustomed to, and stepping out on faith. Before I could do that, I needed to know what was possible, and seriously look at us.

*First the ugly.*

We lived on base, and didn't own a home. I had less than a year left on my contract, and the window to renew it was closing. I didn't have a college degree or a job lined up, and neither did my wife. We also had two young boys to raise, cloth, and feed; and since both of our families were hundreds of miles away, if we stayed put we'd have to do his alone.

*Then the not so bad*

The base that I was assigned to was not far from Savannah, Georgia, a small city with decent number of entry-level jobs. Of course, these jobs would not pay much, but if both of us could get one, we could eat.

The Army owed me money for college for enlisting. It would pay the rent.

My wife and I were only two years away from earning our degrees, and there were three universities nearby. A mind is a terrible thing to waste, and years earlier we made the decision not to waste ours. Best decision we ever made, as completing school would be the key to our success. We were going to stay in the area.

*And the good*

We were all young, healthy, and got along. My relationship with my wife, Gloria, was good, and as long as the kids were taken care of, she would do all that she could.

Over the years, we saved a little money, and we were good at stretching it. Our bills were under control, and our credit was good. And most important since we both qualified for student aid, we could pay for school.

With our chances looking better, we needed to act.

## Act Decisively

For a dream to come true, one has to be decisive, and act quickly. Timing was everything, so if an opportunity presented itself, I was on it. Anything that made life easier was accepted; free classes offered – taken, money offered for school – accepted, and free food - eaten.

One also has to manage perception. I had to be aware of how others saw my plans, and how they saw me achieve them. If seen as indecisive, there would be doubt. Doubt leads to questions about ability, and that'll undermine any plan.

The first real action I took was deciding not to sign a new contract. I caught hell; everyone had something negative to say about my decision. But I was done; soon everyone shut up and acted like they understood.

The next thing I did was focus on getting as much of my college paid for by the Army as I could while I was still employed. Why come out of my pocket? Besides, I'd soon need that money. I enrolled in as many classes as I could handle, and some that I thought that I couldn't; it worked, and in the end, I was able to knock off twelve months of school in less than three, without paying a dime.

I was just getting started, and had a long way to go. To succeed, I really needed to create a plan.

## Developing Your Plan

Honestly, at first I didn't have one; all I had was a vision of how we should be living, and where we needed to be. But as things got rolling and, one fell into place, it dawned on me that the only way for us to regain control over our lives would be through education. We needed to make sure that nothing got between us and earning our college degrees in the limited amount of time that we had.

Managing time was the key, as it was the thing that would keep us in place; so we focused on managing the amount of time that it would take for us to graduate. Since my wife would be done in eighteen months and me just six months later, we used that two-year period as the time-line for the plan. That meant attending school year round, and not creating any new expenses. We had to stay focused and committed.

Just as important as time, was money. I needed a job, but it had to be the right kind of job. A night position or one with odd hours would just stress us all out. The job had to be easy, stable, and stress free; can anyone say *'telemarketing'*? Well that's another story. But it served its' purpose, and gave us the money and benefits we needed to make it through.

Confident, the plan was executed.

## Execute

After committing much time and energy gathering thoughts and crafting a plan, one might assume that the execution would be a snap; it isn't. In fact, for most, it's extremely hard. Why? Because of fear, procrastination, and life.

Fear of being perceived as a failure had held me back many times before. Putting things off and succumbing to life's changes would only make it worse. Knowing this, I had to find a way to ensure that nothing got in our way. It was done through preparation, success, and credibility.

Faced with the fact that we had limited time, limited resources, and no one but us to help us, we had to be prepared for everything. Our credibility was on the line.

We couldn't afford to miss out on an opportunity just because we weren't ready; we always had to be ready to move. We ensured that by finding out everything about what was going on, and being proactive. We couldn't wait for problems to rise up; we smacked them down before they even thought about it. We also created lists for every major thing we had to do; which we checked, double checked, and rechecked. That gave us the ability as needed, and stay focused.

We also earned it through success. Success breeds success, and people are drawn to it. As we progressed, things began to fall into place, people began to take notice, and become more helpful.

My bosses got more flexible with my hours, our teachers more understanding, and believe it or not our creditors more supportive. They actually forgave late payments, waived late fees, and saved our credit!

All of this made the plan more attractive, and removed the doubt. It earned us the credibility we needed when we made mistakes, made life a heck of a lot easier than it could have been, and made it all work.

## Reward Success

Two years later, we were done. We had gone further than we could have possibly imagined, and had finally taken control of our lives.

Each step we took was a milestone, and to keep things interesting, we treated each one as such; treating ourselves to special things as a reward for a job well done. That made our journey much more memorable, more rewarding, and something that we could all look back upon with pride.

*The same can work for you. Lead yourself, and you'll be amazed by the success that follows.*

*–Hassan*

Lisa Panarello

Lisa Panarello is the founder and CEO of *Careers Advance Consulting* and serves as career coach, workshop developer, professional speaker, resume writer, job search trainer and mentor.

Lisa was born in Brooklyn, NY and dreamed of becoming an art director, raising a family, becoming a teacher, and performing on stage. Without being educated in the art of career planning, resume writing, job searching and interviewing, nor privy to the realities of 'on-the-job' expectations, Lisa achieved her dreams with organizations such as *Golden Books, Colgate and Baruch College.*

In order to help others do the same in today's competitive arena, Lisa launched a career development firm to provide professional coaching on the fundamental and progressive tools needed to survive any job market. Since then, Lisa has created over 2,000 results-generating resumes and helped hundreds of clients turn frustrating job search campaigns into exciting career journeys.

Simultaneously, Lisa has presented to hundreds of schools nationwide through CAC and with Monster's *Making It Count!* Organization.

Today, Lisa partners with guidance counselors, college advisors and PTAs to develop and deliver career-preparedness workshops that increase our youth's chances for success wherever they choose to go.

To book a truley exciting, motivational and educational event, program or service, call America's MVP coach.

**Lisa Panarello**
**Careers Advance Consulting**
(718) 605-2290 / lpanarello@si.rr.com
**www.careersadvance.com**

# GET YOUR RPMs IN GEAR
## For the choices that will shape your life.

I'm not sure if I was 'born to be' a leader, but I do know when I 'chose' to become a leader—a leader of me.

*I was 16 years old and filling out my college application. While pondering what major to choose, my brother (a freshman in college at the time) walked by and said, "Why don't you study advertising? You love to write and draw and you're always criticizing commercials." In a split second, I had a vision.*

*I could create magazine ads and direct TV commercials. I could climb the corporate ladder in the Big Apple. I could get married, raise a family and then become a teacher. And someday, somehow I would perform on stage (my twin brother and I used to joke about running off to Hollywood). I pictured myself 10, 20, 30 and 40 years from then and absolutely loved what I saw. I just had to make it happen. So, I made the decision to take a leadership position for life—my life.*

**I didn't know it then, but that decision paved the way for a momentous, adventurous, self-fulfilled career life.**

*My family moved us to Florida in my senior year of high school, but I wasn't going to give up my dreams. I attended community college, worked in my family's Pizzeria restaurant, and two years later, with 48 credits and some savings, I headed back to New York where I pursued a marketing career and progressed to my art director dream job. Three years ago I founded my own business where I currently serve as CEO and Senior Career Consultant. Today, I develop and deliver career-preparedness training workshops for high schools and colleges and travel nationwide as Professional Speaker and Speaker Trainer. Last year I was an extra on the set of an upcoming Steven Speilberg movie and just six months ago I began performing stand-up comedy.*

I'm not sharing these stories just to tell a story. My goal is to illustrate that when you envision a future and take advantage of opportunities that relate to your skills, interests and goals, you CAN make dreams a reality.

Did I know exactly how my life would unfold? Of course not. Did it take a lot of work to get there? Sure. Were there challenges, risks and mistakes along the way? Absolutely. But it was all worth it. By staying in touch with my dreams, I never felt stuck in a dead-end job—I always considered myself 'self-employed'.

## How do you lead yourself to your dreams?

## GET YOUR RPMs IN GEAR
### *For the Decisions that Shape Your Life*

## R = Research and Risk

Wherever you are in life, STOP. Stop and ask yourself: Am I happy? What am I happy about? What would make me happy?

I believe, as many others do, that our jobs and careers do not define who we are. However, they are a large part of our existence and serve as a means to satisfy life interests, personal goals, and of course financial objectives.

Therefore, it's important to consider jobs and careers that:
- Use and/or develop preferred skills—those you want to perform.
- Allow for exploration/advancement in your field(s) of interest.

- Operate in locations and environments you feel most comfortable (i.e. city, country, indoors, outdoors, office, lab, slow, rapid, etc.), and

- Provide for your immediate needs and long term financial goals.

Most people fear the dreaded interview questions "Tell me about yourself?" and "Where do you see yourself in X years?" mostly because they haven't asked themselves these questions nor given their career life the time and thought it deserves. Let's give it some thought with this self-research activity:

---

### Create Your Own 'Dream Job' Description

On a sheet of paper, create three columns. In the first column, list all the things you love about your current and/or previous jobs (i.e. functions, work environments, people, company cultures, growth possibilities, compensation, travel, work hours, location, etc.). In the center, list what you don't like about your current and/or previous jobs. In the last column, list industries, positions and functions you're interested in, even if you don't know much about them yet. With this self-research, you now have a basis for exploring your next career move.

---

Once you have your vision on paper, you can begin to identify opportunities that fit your job description, at least in part. From personal experience, I know that no job is perfect. We may even accept an unwanted job offer simply because we need the money. That does not mean dreams have to be foregone. No job is a waste of time if you take something from it. It's all a matter of what you need.

## For example:

*I was 19 and living with my brothers in Brooklyn. A year later the company decided to relocate to New Jersey and I opted out of that 2-hour commute. After two months of pounding the pavement, I was offered a job in a financial brokerage firm. I had no real interest, but needed to pay the bills, so I accepted. Six months later I received a $3,000 raise and $2,000 bonus.*

*I knew this job was way off my career path and that I wouldn't graduate college in the traditional time frame. Yet, I also knew that I'd be working in the exciting, fast-paced environment I was suited for while earning a progressive salary. My fellow brokers said I would never leave the money. Six years later I finished my degree, secured an internship—at the age of 26—and launched my marketing career with a 60% pay cut.*

I made these choices by weighing risks against rewards as they related to my goals. What are you willing to do to achieve your dreams? What are you not willing to do? Compromise and sacrifice do come into play, but they should be at levels that work for *you,* not the hiring company.

We all want to impress interviewers and hear the words "you're hired." However, prior to pursuing a job and before you say "I accept" (to working 8-12 hours/day), take the time to research if the company, industry and position are a right fit for you at that time and can help lead you to where you want to go. In real estate, it's location, location, location. In career development, it's research, research, research. With that, you can then take the next step.

### P = Plan and Prioritize

Most of us would gladly take the time to plan a two-week vacation or that once in lifetime wedding day. Why not take the time to plan your work-life future? Does that mean everyone should have a 40 year plan? Of course not. However, thinking ahead allows you to back out the steps needed to get there. While many people feel it's all about luck (a.k.a. being at the right place at the right time), if you keep your eyes and ears open while working hard to pursue your dreams, YOU will put yourself in the right place at the right time.

### For instance:

*I wanted to become an art director, but didn't want to go the route of a graphic designer. So, I chose the broad field of marketing as a way to pursue my creative interests. From that decision forward, I made sure I put myself in the path of creative people and functions related to my 'dream job' description. Within one year I turned my role as marketing assistant into project manager responsible for sales material development. When the art director resigned, I had the experience and relationships to take over (and I had still never touched graphic design software).*

**Planning does not bring guarantees. It fosters confident decision making and reduces the risks of wasted time, energy and money.**

Let's say you want to pursue a career in real estate or financial sales and you have no interest in going to a four-year college. It would be helpful to know that there are license and certificate programs available that jump start these careers.

On the flip side, if you're unsure of what career to pursue, think about what you like to do in your spare time and test drive careers by taking a course or volunteering.

At minimum, conduct internet research and talk over your ideas with counselors and industry professionals. These activities can provide valuable information and real-life perspectives—while building referral networks!

When you combine short term planning with the simplest of self/market research, you can significantly impact your opportunities for immediate success. And if you prioritize your plan for the long run, you're in for a journey towards satisfying your highest priorities.

**For example:**

*A retail store manager decided she wanted to move out of New York and raise a famil. To prepare for this big change we used self/market research to create her new 'ideal scene' on paper and identified careers that fit her interests, skill sets, location preference and compensation needs. Then we set a plan for acquiring the skills/educational requirements necessary for these careers and building relationships in her cities of choice.*

I'm not trying to make light of anyone's personal situation. Life is rarely simple. We all have challenges to face, albeit personal or job-related, that can make it harder to achieve. However, they can be overcome, some even avoided. Dreams can be secured with the right amount of information, planning, commitment and support.

In addition, contingency planning can help. Along your career journey if you learn a progressive skill, attend industry seminars/courses and maintain professional/mentoring networks, *you will help yourself* survive unforeseen workplace pitfalls while preparing for desired *and* unexpected opportunities.

Okay, so research will help you identify goals and a well-designed plan will visualize the means to achieve. But how do you actually reach the finish line? You get the last of your RPMs in gear.

## M = Market and Manage

There is no way around it. To make your dream career a reality, you have to market it, sell it and own it.

I was fortunate to have figured out my career future at such a young age, but it wasn't until three years ago that I realized how lucky I was to have lived in simpler times.

*At 19 I wrote my first resume. It was apparently good enough to work with local employment agencies. My speaking skills must have impressed employers, because I secured my first three jobs with just one interview each, way before I earned my degree. Six years later, I changed careers from brokerage to marketing—overnight. Throughout the next four years, I conducted several job search campaigns and secured multiple, simultaneous job offers in different industries.*

Today we live in a highly competitive job market where millions of jobs are posted on the internet with thousands of people applying to the same one—and the interview process can last two, three, even four or more meetings. It's challenging to say the least.

While I didn't know what I was doing right at the time, I don't believe my successes happened by accident. In fact, the basic keys to my success are the very keys that can open doors in any job market:

- Commitment to dreams and focus on the work ahead.
- Confidence in the capacity to learn and ability to be flexible.
- Mentors and professional resources; and last but not least,
- Stand-out, tailored resumes to break the ice time and time again.

Over the years I redeveloped my resume to fit different opportunities. Today, I possess 18 versions. Does everyone *need* that many? That depends on your past experiences and future job goals. However, everyone needs at least one dynamic, brief, detailed, creative, results-oriented master resume.

If you possess strong writing skills and/or are willing to work with resume tutorials, create your own masterpiece. If not, find a friend who can help. And to be sure your resume will survive the competitive job market, have it reviewed by a professional. They can both critique and prepare stand-out resumes and can educate you on how to progress and manage them toward any career idea or job need. It's well worth the investment to have that critical sales tool ready to market and the power to customize it at a moment's notice.

### Don't wait to be great. Get your RPMs in Gear Today!

Whether you are seeking to jump start, maintain, advance or change your career/job situation, it's going to take time to make it happen, so relieve some future pressure and get started now.

**R**esearch yourself, your risk tolerance and your market
**P**lan and prioritize your next series of career moves
**M**arket and manage yourself toward your dreams

Two other keys to success, in my opinion, are a sense of humor and staying clear of negativity—those who say "it can't happen".

If you sit behind the wheel of your dreams, map out the roads to get there, keep eyes open for alternate routes and passionately drive your plans with the right tools and resources, I guarantee that you can achieve a self-designed life—it's the best feeling in the world!

**Choose to become a leader of your career and your life.**
**With an RPM strategy, anything is possible!**

Thank you and good luck in all that you dream.

Matt B. Kuennen

Matt B. Kuennen is an established leader in the banking industry. He has ten years of banking experience that has propelled him to a Vice President and Sales Development Consultant position inside a fortune 500 company. He has been involved in thousands of discussions and delivered many speeches on management techniques. As a Non-Profit foundation board member he has extended his natural leadership abilities to the local community in which he lives. Matt has been involved with the Sacramento Kings as a youth team captain coordinator on several occasions and has a passion for Basketball.

**e-mail: skuennen@surewest.net**

**Phone: 916-801-9645**

# LEADERSHIP 5.0:
# Five leadership principles for today's Manager

In order for you to advance as a leader you have to know that the one constant in business and life, is change. Who ever can accept, process, implement and adapt the fastest to this constant change has the competitive advantage that every organization looks for in a manager. As a leader, everyone turns to you during times of change for direction, structure, confidence, motivation or the short version LEADERSHIP. The true leader stands out not when things are running smooth but when adversity has been placed in there path. In order to be an effective leader you need to have a set of basic principles that drive every decision you make. Every leader has different ideas on how they approach certain situations. These principles are your guideposts through the difficulties that arise in life or business.

In this chapter you will learn about my experience with leading people and the principles I apply to my business dealings.

## Vision

When I first started as a manager I remember being confident yet nervous about the thought of people looking to me to make decisions. It didn't help that a lot of the people who would be following my direction were older then me. I learned very quickly that in order to get others to follow I had to learn how to lead, and fast. No matter what your leadership roll is it's vital to have a clear VISION of the goals you and your team are trying to accomplish. This VISION that you maintain as a leader will help you to organize your thoughts and keep you focused when others might fall astray. Your Vision might not be a single idea, but an ideology of how you want everything around you to function.

## First Things First

Stop whatever you are doing right now. Go get some paper and a pencil. Then go somewhere quiet and secluded. This will allow you to step out of your day-to-day routine. Begin brainstorming and writing down what you would like to accomplish in your roll as a leader. For example, when I did this exercise, one of the pieces I came up with was coaching and development of others. For me mentoring others to learn and grow in their work is important because I like to help other people be successful. Don't worry if you have a lot of stuff written on the paper, the idea is to get all of it out in front of you. Your VISION should align somewhat with the company that you work for.

Your Vision should have the five following ingredients to ensure it has impact on you and your team.

1 – An Ideal Purpose
2 – It should be unique
3 – It should portray an Image of how you want to be seen by others
4 – It should be future oriented
5 – It should have a common purpose in mind

Now that you have gathered your thoughts, it's time for you to come up with your VISION of what you would like to accomplish as a leader. Take that VISION back to your team. In order to make that vision a success you will have to ensure that your team is engaged with what they will have to do. It is important to have the rest of the team's VISION aligned with yours. Any great leader is open to people questioning there motive. Your VISION might change slightly to adjust to the goals of the team.

## Command

If you have your VISION lined with a clear view of what you want to accomplish, you are ready to motivate your team to success. In order for you and your team to be successful there will have to be some changes. These changes will call for difficult decisions. A lot of times, as a leader, decisions have to be made in an instant. In making those split second decisions you have to be confident in your resolve. With that said, your staff will not only have to TRUST that you have made the right decision, they will have to carry out your decisions as if they were their own. COMMAND is such a key principle because it requires directness. Most managers will struggle with this crucial leadership principle because they want everyone to look at them as a great person. The tendancy of most mangers is to hope everyone likes them, instead of ensuring they are respected. Directness sometimes can be extremely harsh. There are three aspects to the COMMAND skill that will have impact on your staff.

*#1 – Command their respect* – This one may sound easy, but it's harder then most people think. Respect is earned through hard work and discipline. Another way to say that is LEAD BY EXAMPLE. People will not follow what you say, until they see what you can do.

*#2 – Command Their communication* – Now that they see you will walk the walk, get them to talk. The #1 reason teams are dysfunctional is because they simply don't communicate. I'm sure most teams will say they communicate well. You might even be saying to yourself that your team communicates well. That may be true, however just remember that you can never over communicate.

*#3 – Command their activities* – * Warning – For 75% of the managers out there you might want to sit down for this. Command your employee's activities, do not manage their results. Any body can wear a nice name tag that says manager and ask their employees at the end of the day "did you make quota today"? A true leader with a command character manages the activities throughout the day. The COMMAND leader will help structure those activities for the day, week, and month to ensure success through strategy.

When you apply these three rules to your current leadership style you will have a more consistently productive staff which produces redults.

## Coaching

Now that you have plotted your vision for your team and established a firm command, start coaching to the effectiveness of your team. In order for your team members to flourish in there positions they need more then the occasional offsite training class. Knowledge of products will only get you so far. It's all in how they deal with customers and each other. The one person who should be talking with your employees more then their customers is you. As the manger in the office you should not only be the best, but expect your employees to act and do as you would, even when you are not there. You have to dedicate a very large portion of your time to team member development. This time can be spent in several different ways, below are some of the more effective examples for coaching team members:

- *Weekly Team Meetings* – This is a great forum to not only have open COMMUNICATION, but to discuss different ideas of what is working to develop business and what is not working.

- *Instant coach* – One of my favorite. This is usually when you see your employees in there truest form. Just drop by and observe them during a business transaction with a client. You can really give valuable feedback from these interactions.

  - Pay less attention to what your people are saying and more attention to what they are doing.

- *Pre-positioned coaching.* – This is an opportunity to prepare with your team member what type of activities should occur during an upcoming appointment or meeting. You should focus on high impact questions to help your staff self-discover how they can have the most success. Some questions might sound like, "What is the expected outcome of the meeting?" "what will you do if this situation happens?" What would be the impact on the client if you did that?"

- *One-on-One coaching* – There are two ways to handle these coaching sessions. Both of which are used to help team members to become more effective with customer interactions.

  *#1 – Self Discovering* – Allow your team member to determine on their own what they could have done different to be more successful in the encounter. Then work with them to apply those findings to future transactions.

*#2 – Telling* – Tell the employee what concerned you about the customer interaction or what you really liked about the interaction. You want to ensure that most of the time you are applying the Self – Discovery method when you are coaching.

These coaching techniques can be applied to produce more sales, better customer service, enhance team member communication, or used when dealing with other managers or coworkers.

## Accountability

The single biggest downfall of any leader is not having the ability to hold people accountable; this sometimes will include your self. Accountability can often be mistaken as punitive or negative. This is why many leaders fail to keep their teams engaged. There comes a time when you have to hold someone accountable because they have failed to achieve or perform at a certain level. As, long as you have lived up to Managing there activities and coaching them to be more effective, they should not be surprised by the ACCOUNTABILITY. Refer back to your rule #1 in the COMMAND principle. COMMAND THER RESPECT. If you fail to hold your team members accountable for there actions or lack there of you will fail as a leader to the rest of the team. Once you have allowed underachieving performers to go unchecked it is difficult to gain your credibility as a leader back.

## Recognition

This principle applies in every facet of life. It can be used with team members, family members, friends, your manager, or even a stranger. The ability to recognize others publicly and personally is indicative with great leaders. One thing to remember when you are applying the above mentioned principles is that people work for you not the company. So when a team member meets or exceeds your excpectations, while staying true to the team VISION, it is imperative that you recognize them for their accomplishments. It has to be heartfelt and specific. Please don't do the generic "thanks for everything you do" speech that comes out once a year during Christmas. You have to be forthcoming with your praise. Praise should not only be in private, but in public around their peers and coworkers. Now you have used you're RECOGNITION principle to keep the whole team engaged because they respect the ability to pass credit to others.

The principles written in this chapter are developed from my years of experience in leading others. I follow these principles daily to ensure that I stay consistent.

I highly recommend that you immediately implement all of the above principles with your team. These principles have proven over the years to be the secret to my success. These principles will only work if you believe in them. Your belief, along with your teams "buy-in" to your VISION of things to come will propel your leadership skills to new heights.

Robin Aikens

Robin Aikens was born on December 26, 1969 in Chicago, Illinois.

Golf was taken up at a young age for Robin. She began playing golf at the age of 6 and at age 7, Robin began competing with The Bob-O-Links Junior golf club a division of the Chicago Women Golf Club. Now she is a member of the Ladies Professional Golf Association (LPGA) Teaching and Club Professional Division. By the time Robin graduated from high school, she had won over 25 trophies and awards for golf. Robin auditioned for Emerson School for Visual and Performing Arts in Gary, Indiana, when she was in the 7th grade, where she majored in violin performance. She was actively involved in playing in the Emerson Symphony orchestra, and she began playing professionally in the Gary Civic Symphony before graduating high school. Robin won 15 first place awards for violin performance (solo and group performance) for the Indiana State School Music Association (ISSMA).

Robin went on to Purdue University and she walked on the Purdue Women's Golf Team. During her college years, she won the Midwest District College Division. Robin did not continue at Purdue West Lafayette Campus. She continued her college experience at Purdue University Calumet in Hammond, Indiana. Robin also played in the Purdue University Symphony Orchestra -1st violin section at Purdue University West Lafayette campus. She has a B.A. from Purdue and (2) Master of Arts Degrees from Roosevelt University. She is currently a doctoral candidate in Organizations Leadership.

Robin is a corporate trainer and motivational speaker and has shared the stage with Les Brown, one of the top 5 speakers in the world. She has written several other books and has her own column with *The Green Magazine* in New York, she is also a contributing writer for the *Savoy Magazine* and *The African American Golfers Digest*.

**By Robin Aikens, LPGA pro**
P.O. Box 178477
Chicago, Illinois 60617

**(866)823-3357 • www.golfsafariproducts.com**

# Finding Your 'Sweet Spot'

When I was approached to write my chapter within this book, I had to go to the core of the topic, "Unleash the Leader Within You." So what is the action of unleashing something? According to The American Heritage Dictionary, unleash means to let go of a cord, chain, or strap that is used to hold something. So that means that we have to let go of that something that is holding us back from leading ourselves. We have that ability to lead ourselves out of something, or to something that we are destined for. That destiny might be to write a book, teach a class, or to start our own business. We have the ability to unleash the leader within ourselves because we are worth it.

The way that I unleashed the leader within me was to reach down in my soul to extract out all of the negative stuff that had been trapped within me. I had to let go of the negative people, negative ideas, and negative state that I had caught myself in over and over again. When I decided to pursue my dream, or my 'magnificent obsession' to become a member of the Ladies Professional Golf Association (LPGA), I had to tear myself down before I would build myself up. My aunt was my babysitter at the time I was trying to become a LPGA teaching professional, and she kept my children for me when I went to work. I would pick her up on Sunday and she would stay all week at my house. She was an excellent babysitter. But, I needed to practice after work in order to pass my test to become a member of the LPGA. However, she told me that she would not watch my children for me even when she stayed there all week. That was a trying time for me because I needed my job, and I needed a babysitter. I had two month old twins and a three year old. A few months before, I had filed papers to divorce my husband because he was unsupportive. So I unleashed the leader within me by tearing down all of the people that were holding me back from obtaining my dream. Eventually, my divorce went through, I fired my aunt, and found another babysitter. I quit my job taking a $45,000 pay cut to pursue my dream. I gave up everything for my dream.

## Finding Your 'Sweet Spot'

According to Frank Thomas, Golf Digest Magazine's Chief Technical Advisor, the 'sweet spot' is the impact point on the golf club where you feel minimum twisting of the club head during or after impact. You can produce desirable shots as long as the club is traveling down the right path and the club face is squared or centered.

In relation to golf, hitting the 'sweet spot' will produce desirable shots as long as you have some other key factors working in your favor. In relation to life, hitting the 'sweet spot' means hitting a target in your life so that you can produce desirable outcomes in your life. The process of hitting your 'sweet spot' on the golf club will produce a percussion point and you can metaphorically hear the club sing. Can you imagine that? What is your 'sweet spot', that something that gets you excited enough to sing about? In relation to life, finding your 'sweet spot' is 'zeroing in' on a target and getting exactly what you have desired from it. That target might be following your dreams, buying a new house, getting a new job, making more money, or making a transition between relationships.

> *"Hold fast to dreams, for if dreams die, life is like a broken-winged bird that cannot fly."*
> **—Langston Hughes**

Finding my 'sweet spot' was becoming a member of The Ladies Professional Golf Association (LPGA). There were various stages that led up to that. At age six, my mom enrolled me in junior golf lessons. At age 7, I began to compete with other young people and I joined the Bob-O-Links Junior Golf Club in Chicago. At the end of that summer, I won a trophy in the club's Championship tournament. During the summers, we had weekly golf lessons at Jackson Park Golf Course on the south side of Chicago. Every Monday, we played competitively against each other. During the winter months, we had indoor golf lessons. My first golf instructor was Mr. Booker Blair. I remember Mr. Blair making me stand in the correct posture for hours it seemed. However, it paid off. If he were alive today, he would be proud of my accomplishments.

We had two tournaments amongst club members in the summers. One was in the beginning of the summer. It was called the Warm-Up Tournament. The other tournament was toward the end of the summer. It was called the Championship Tournament. The members of the Bob-O-Links competed against other golf clubs in the Midwest. The tournaments were hosted in different cities in the summer. It was called the Midwest District Junior Golf Tournament. I won this tournament three times. I have also won over twenty-five titles playing junior golf.

The summer of my fourth grade year, my mom got remarried and we moved to Gary, Indiana. I continued to commute to Chicago for golf lessons. I also played at the neighborhood course in Gary. My passion for the game led me to play golf in high school where I was named MVP the years that I played. I played golf at Roosevelt High School in Gary. I attended Emerson School for Visual and Performing Arts in that same city. I majored in violin performance. Emerson did not have any sports. After I graduated, I continued my education at Purdue University.

While attending Purdue University in West Lafayette, Indiana, I was a walk-on to The Purdue University Women's Golf Team. I had to practice some shots and play a round of golf to prove to the coach that I could play. I was the only African American on my team. However, it was a great feeling to be given a golf bag that said Purdue University Women's Golf.

As I grew older, I would watch the LPGA Tour on television. I always said to myself that I wanted to become a professional golfer. Now that I am a member of the LPGA Teaching and Club Professional Division, I look back over my life and say, "Wow, look where I came from." Thanks to the dedication of my mom, I was able to attend lessons and tournaments. Also, I would like to thank a man named "Cakes" for inspiring me to become professional. He would attend pro events with me. Julius Richardson, one of Golf Magazine's Top 100 teachers, has been coaching me for over eight years.

As a young girl, I would listen to people who were my elders. I would hear them say, "I could have done this," or "I should have done that." They were referring to their dreams. I always wondered, "Well, why didn't you?" "What held you back?" These questions were never answered. I still have those questions today.

What is keeping you from your dreams? Is it fear, or anxiety? Does it mean that you must move out of your comfort zone? Do you have the courage to change your condition? Are you proactive?

*"Being proactive is more that taking initiative. It is recognizing that we are responsible for our own choices and have the freedom to choose based on principles and values rather than on moods or conditions. Proactive people are agents of change and choose not to be victims, or reactive, or blame others."*
**—Stephen R. Covey**

You must be proactive in order to follow your dreams or to find your 'sweet spot'. You must also be prepared for your opportunity.

*"I think luck is preparation meeting opportunity."*
**—Pete Rose**

I think that I have been lucky at times, but I also believe that opportunities came as a result of me being focused on what I wanted out of life.

*"If you fail in life, try to land on your back because if you can look up, you can get up."*
**–Les Brown**

## Your 'Sweet Spot'

What is the process of finding your 'sweet spot'? First of all, you must ask yourself, "What is my magnificent obsession?" "What do I do best, or what do I love?" What brings you joy, or gets you excited? What brings out the percussion point in you? Is it singing, dancing, making pottery, working on computers, fixing cars, cleaning houses, or playing sports. These things can produce happiness and possibly bring you much success. You may encounter many defeats and setbacks through the process of finding your 'sweet spot". That's OK! That's apart of the growth process. Make sure that you are specific about what you want out of life. Often times, people fail because they don't know what they want from life. Some people go through life indecisive. Just be committed to whatever you want, and success will follow.

For instance, before a missile is aimed at a target, the person launching the missile must know exactly where the missile is to go. It is the same with your dreams, or your 'sweet spot'. You must know exactly what you are aiming in order to hit your target.

Now you might ask, "Well how do I know what is my 'sweet spot'?" Many times when I train people, I tell them it is your gut instinct telling you what it is that you love. Some call it your 'still small voice.' Most people uncover this while meditating or being in a quiet place. Go to that place where you can be at peace. If you have children, wait until they are asleep and meditate, go to a library or the beach. Wherever you can find peace and tranquility, go to that place. Take a journal with you and write notes to yourself. Post your dreams on your refrigerator, wall, or mirror in your bathroom. See it constantly, and act on it!

What gets you excited or motivated to do magnificent things? What do you think about constantly? Besides spending time with friends and family, what mark would you leave on earth if you had only one year to live. Would you set up a foundation for children, would you set up a homeless shelter, would you record a song, would you start a business to continue your legacy on to your family? More than likely, this is your dream. This is what you are passionate about. When you are passionate about something, your adrenaline begins to flow. When your adrenaline begins to flow, you become energized, motivated to make a move on your dreams. Sometimes the fire will die out, but it is up to you to keep the fire going. You must ignite the fire within you. Don't worry about how you are going to do it. Money and resources are not an issue. When you find your 'sweet spot' or your magnificent obsession, the help and the resources will come to you. You will see that the universe will yield to you.

Continue to strive to unleash the leader within you! You can do it and it is a process that you must go through. However, once you unleash the leader within you, you will start working on levels that will literally amaze you.

(This is an excerpt from the book, "How I Found My 'Sweet Spot'... and How You Can Find Yours" by Robin Aikens. You can order the book by logging on to www.golfsafariproducts.com.)

## The results of finding my 'Sweet Spot'

In 1998, I formed Inner City Golf, a 501 C3 non-profit Corporation to teach disadvantaged youth how to play the game of golf. Since then, I have won 2 awards for Inner City Golf. In 2000, the organization won the S. Gary Oniki Award for Community Empowerment from the Community Renewal Society. In 2001, Inner City Golf won the Hook A Kid on Golf "New Program of the Year Award." In 2002, the program made history by bringing the first ever all-girls team to its Traditions of Golf Challenge in Valporaiso, Indiana. Program participants were on hand to watch Michael Jordan conduct a golf clinic at The Merit Club in Gurnee, Illinois. Two female participants played a round of golf with touring pro, Jennifer RoSales at The Kellogg-Keebler Pro-Am at Stonebridge Country Club.

Robin has walked 18 holes with Michael Jordan, as his walking scorer for his celebrity Golf Invitational in Paradise Island, Bahamas. She has conducted numerous golf clinics for corporations and celebrities. One of the golf clinics she conducted was for Earvin "Magic" Johnson for his celebrity golf tournament in Los Angeles, California.

Robin continues to carry her message through her motivational speeches and corporate training. This former Miss America contestant has shared the stage with Les Brown, one of the top 5 speakers in the world. She shares her message with thousands at universities, such as Purdue University. Schools throughout the country and corporate trainings. Robin has her own column with *The Green Magazine* in New York, called *"The*

*Finer Points."* She is also a contributing writer for the *Savoy Magazine* and *The African American Golfers Digest.*

Robin will launch her own golf apparel line in Spring 2006 with her supplier in Taipei, Tawain. She will come out with her first CD, playing the violin, in 2007. She is an actress and has appeared in several movies, television programs, and has done numerous radio interviews. Robin has been a guest host on 102.3 FM in Chicago. This is ultimately what happened to me by finding my 'sweet spot' and *Unleashing the Leader Within Me!*

To book Robin Aikens for corporate training or motivational speaking, please log on to www.golfsafariproducts.com or call (866) 823-3357 or (773) 410-1621.

Rosa Williams Sherk

Rosa Williams Sherk is an award-winning trainer, author, coach and motivational speaker who has successfully helped thousands of individuals enhance their skills and improve their self-esteem. Through her company-Mirror Training and Consulting, she has become known to many as the "Mirror Lady" because of her passion and commitment to helping others create larger visions of themselves. As the message behind the message that she brings, she has inspired countless individuals to see themselves doing far more than they ever dreamed.

As a trainer holding numerous professional certifications from some of the world's leading Train-the-Trainer organizations such as Langevin Learning Services, Achieve Global, and Development Dimensions International (DDI), Rosa has traveled across the country speaking and training Managers, Engineers, Technicians, Customer Service Representatives and call centers employees.

Speaking on topics such as coping with changing, diversity, customer service leadership, and goal-setting, Rosa is in high demand because of her unique ability to connect with people on all levels and help companies reach their organizational goals.

Rosa is a member of Toastmaster International and the Les Brown Speaker Network. She also has a background in Electrical Engineering as well as a degree in the behavioral sciences.

You may **contact Rosa Williams Sherk** through her website: **www.rosasherk.com**, by e-mail at **aspire@rosasherk.com**, or by phone at **919-293-0040**

# Dare To Lead

Today, I want to challenge you to do something that will change your life forever. I want you to find a mirror right now and take a long hard look at the person staring back at you. There is greatness in that person. Yes, I mean there is greatness in YOU!

Perhaps you've never thought of yourself as a leader. Ryan White probably didn't start out thinking of himself as a leader either. Ryan was a hemophiliac who spent most of the first five or six years of his life in and out of hospitals. In 1984 at the age of thirteen, during a blood transfusion, he contracted AIDS. The world did not know then what we know now about AIDS. In addition to the physical pain associated with the hemophilia, Ryan endured painful humiliation and discrimination from children and adults alike. Through all of his suffering he maintained a positive attitude and emerged a leader and challenged the world to redefine how we view people with AIDS. Instead of suffering in silence, he became the public face of AIDS. To educate the world and bring attention to AIDS, he appeared on TV talk shows, news magazines, and even spoke before the President's Commission on AIDS. Although Ryan only lived 19 years, in his short lifetime, he unleashed the leader from within and the world stood up and listened. As a society, we became more educated about AIDS and the stigma of the disease gave way to treating people with AIDS more humanely.

Although I feel as though I knew Ryan White personally, I did not, nor do I personally know anyone with AIDS. Yet, Ryan touched my life because I am part of humanity, and he made the world more humane.

There was greatness in Ryan and I believe that there is greatness in all of us. I challenge you today not to be defined by your age, weight, height, race, financial status nor by what others say about you. There is a leader inside waiting to be uncovered. This day, I challenge you to unleash the leader within YOU.

## 1. Take the Journey of Self-Discovery

Self-knowledge and self-awareness are two areas that you want to explore on this journey. Remember, leadership is about influence. So, before you can effectively influence others in the direction you want them to go, you must know whom you are and where you want to go. Know your authentic self. Effective leaders model the behaviors they want others to demonstrate. You must know what your values are in order to model a firm commitment to your values and beliefs. Invest some quiet, committed time exploring your heart, spirit and mind to clarify what your values are and what "truth" is to you. Do this in order that you can be true to yourself and to others. Shakespeare said it best in Hamlet:

> *This above all: to thine own self be true,*
> *And it must follow, as the night the day,*
> *Thou canst not then be false to any man.*

Two other key attributes of an effective leader are purpose and vision. As you continue on your journey of self-discovery you will be able to determine your purpose in life. That is why this journey of self-discovery is so vitally important.

What is your purpose in life? Why are you here? Identify your purpose by becoming aware of what you are passionate about. What would you do 365 days a year, 24 hours a day if you could? Discover what really gives your life meaning. Psychiatrist, psychologist and philosopher Dr. Viktor E. Frankl, after being a prisoner in the German death camps in 1942, wrote about his personal experiences and his observations in a powerful book entitled, Man's Search for Meaning. Because of those experiences and observations, he adopted the philosophy that *a man can live only so far as he has a meaning in his life.* **What gives your life meaning?**

From my own personal experience, I can tell you that the search for meaning on the journey of self- discovery will not be easy; but the pay-off will be huge!

Before I took the journey of self-discovery, I recalled feeling like I was just floundering. I was being pulled in many different directions. Some friends were telling me I should be in engineering because I liked math, others were telling me that I should be a lawyer because I was diplomatic and in their opinion, a good debater. I tried electrical engineering and although it was a great field that paid a lot of money, it was not my passion. It was just a job.

I decided to embark on a journey of self-discovery to find my voice. All I knew at that time was that I cared deeply about people and that it was important to me to encourage people to realize their self-worth and stretch beyond that which was comfortable for them. I was very passionate about making people feel special regardless of their age, sex, race, profession or socioeconomic status. I guess I felt so strongly about that because I had grown up poor, but I knew that poverty did not define me. I knew that there was a servant of mankind waiting to be unleashed in me and that the same was true of so many others. They simply needed someone to believe in them. I wanted to be that someone.

This led me to the field of training and development. Over the years in training, I grew as a leader. I became so passionate about training that my reputation spread throughout the company and my feedback evaluation almost always contained comments about my passion and how inspired the participants were by being in my class. I could not take credit for the way lives were being impacted. The credit belongs to the gift. *Every good and perfect gift comes from above (James 1:17.)* You see, we all have a gift. We just have to find our voice. I had found my voice and by following my passion, I became a master trainer and accepted the responsibility of training other trainers not just to lead, but to lead from the heart.

The pay-off for taking that journey of self-discovery led me to a place of peace and fulfillment. I found a life full of meaning and purpose. Today, as a trainer, speaker, coach and author, I am still humbled by the responsibility that life has charged me with-helping others find their voice. I am a servant of mankind. The journey of self-discovery led me to this place. I dare you to take the journey and unleash the leader within YOU!

## 2. Be a Person of Strong Character

People of strong character demonstrate the attributes of self-discipline, honesty, trustworthiness, courage, commitment, strength, determination and dependability. A lack of these attributes can undermine trust in you as a leader. As Socrates once said, *"The undisciplined life is an insane life."* No one wants to follow one who is insane.

Leaders do not demand respect; they earn respect. Margaret Thatcher said, "Being a leader is a lot like being a lady-if you have to tell people that you are, you are not."

You earn respect as a leader in several ways. One way is by being ethical and above reproach in all deeds at all times. This is why the self-discovery journey that we talked about earlier is so important. You must be committed to your values and beliefs. This is especially true in the most challenging moments. People will not follow you if they do not see the commitment in you. It has been said, "Character builds slowly, but it can be torn down with incredible swiftness."

Additionally, you earn respect by going where you want others to follow. Leaders do not stand back and give orders. Leaders lead the charge. Leaders do not ask others to do what they will not do. I dare you to have the strength of character to unleash the leader within you and model the way for others to follow!

## 3. Create Synergy Through a Shared Vision

People who share in a common vision can achieve goals a lot quicker and a lot easier than others because they move in the same direction. Their shared-vision creates synergy.

Synergy is the combined effect of everyone's efforts where one plus one does not equal two, but rather one plus one equals far more. Geese know this principle well. They know that they can fly so much further together

---

in "V" formation than each goose can fly independently. Researchers discovered that geese fly in "V" formation because as each bird flaps its wings, it creates uplift for the bird flying directly behind it. By flying this way the entire flock adds a minimum of 71% greater flying range.

Geese work together toward a common goal. Leaders champion a common cause. Whatever cause you decide to champion as a result of your self-discovery journey, you will attract others. Share your vision and be committed to it. You will see the vision spread from the spark in your heart to the hearts of others. Show that you care. Remember, people do not care how much you know until they know how much you care.

The true story of the Greensboro Four is an excellent example of how creating synergy can bring about powerful results when the elements of purpose, vision, planning and character are present.

One February day in 1960, four A&T State University freshmen changed the course of history. Joseph McNeil, Ezell Blair, Jr. David Richmond and Frank McCain were tired of the dehumanizing disrespect black people received in the segregated South. They simply wanted *equality.*

Joseph McNeil's breaking point occurred when he was denied service at a Union Bus Station terminal in Greensboro, North Carolina. McNeil shared this experience with his roommate and two other friends upon returning to his college dormitory. As a result, they all concluded that something had to be done.

The four freshmen came up with the *plan* of a peaceful sit-in at the Woolworth's lunch counter. Woolworth's was a five and dime store where black people were allowed to shop, but not allowed to sit at the lunch counter to eat. These four young men were *committed* to their cause and their principle of non-violence even when bystanders spit on them and called them names.

Within a couple of days female students from Bennett College and a number of white students for nearby University of North Carolina at Greensboro, joined the sit-ins. By the 5th day the number of student protesters at

Woolworth's had grown to three hundred and the sit-in movement had begun to take place in forty other cities in the South. Like all effective leaders, David, Frank, Ezell and Joseph had duplicated themselves. The *synergy* among the students could not be ignored as the movement gained *momentum*.

As a result of these four ordinary individuals who dared to lead, others caught the vision and segregation in the South was brought to its knees.

I dare you to spark a shared vision and unleash the leader within YOU!

## 4. Engage in Continuous Improvement

Even though some people appear to have natural gifts and talents, people are not born leaders-leaders develop over time. John Maxwell put it best when he said, "Becoming a leader is a lot like investing successfully in the stock market. If your hope is to make a fortune in a day, you're not going to be successful."

Let's compare being a leader to the stock market for a moment. If you know anything at all about the stock market, you know that it goes up and down. The key to being successful in the market is to make systematic investments over long periods of time. Even when the market is not doing well, smart investors continue to invest because they know that it is during those times that they can really pick up some valuable stocks at lower prices. They know that winning in the stock market requires a constant re-evaluation of their stock portfolio as they continue to add stocks of value.

Similarly, the ability to lead is a process of acquiring skills and continuously refining those skills. Often it is through the most challenging times of our lives that we refine our character and grow the most. Like smart investors, we hold fast to what Dr. Robert Schuller, pastor of the famed Crystal Cathedral Church in Garden Grove California said, "Tough times never last, tough people do." I dare you to commit to continuous improvement and unleash the leader within YOU!

## 5. Pay the Rent

The world needs you and your unique gifts. There are things to be accomplished that will not be accomplished if you do not do them. You see, we all showed up on earth with a purpose. Someone's answer to their situation depends upon you living out your purpose. There is a book waiting to be written that only you can write; a song to be sung like only you can sing, a masterpiece to be painted that only you can paint, a cure to be discovered, a child to be mentored, a company to be built like only you build. These things will never grace our world unless you live out your purpose for being here. Henry David Thoreau said, *"Oh, God, to reach the point of death, only to realize that you've never lived, only to realize that you've never scraped the surface of your potential."*

Oh, what a tragedy in life!

The world needs the service of effective leaders. It has been said, *"Service is the rent that we pay for our time here on earth."*

I encourage you to pay the rent and unleash the leader within YOU!

Right now as you stare in the mirror, I want to encourage you to get started on your journey of self-discovery. Like my coach and mentor, Les Brown says, "You don't have to be great to get started, but you do have to get started to be great. There is greatness in YOU!

**I DARE YOU TO UNLEASH THE LEADER WITHIN YOU!**

Shanita B. Akintonde

Shanita B. Akintonde, MBA, ATM-B, is a college professor, wife, mother, motivational speaker, author, doctoral student, soul food connoisseur, and businesswoman. As Cheif Visionary Officer of Creative Notions Group Inc., Shanita travels across the country motivating students, professional organizations, and business entities on the topics of higher education access, leadership, communication, career transition, and work/life balance. Known as "The College Success Expert," Shanita is a major presenter at conferences such as Monster Diversity Leadership Weekend, Toastmasters International Leadership Institute and a highly successful college career conference that she coordinates called ADSTOCK. To date, her motivational messages have reached over 100,000 audience members across 25 states. In 2004, she was ranked as one of the top three speakers for Monster's Making High School Count program by counselors, academic advisors and students.

Shanita earned a BA degree in advertising from Columbia College Chicago, an MBA in marketing and organizational development from Illinois Institute of Technology, and is a current doctoral student in higher education, leadership, and counseling psychology at Loyola University Chicago. In addition, she has obtained certification in advanced advertising studies from University of Illinois—Champaign-Urbana and media planning from McDonald's Hamburger University.

She is a member of The American Assoiciation of University Women, The National MBA Association, The American Marketing Association, Toastmasters International, The Public Relations Society of America, The Saint Sabina School Board, Alpha Kappa Alpha Sorority, Inc. and Top Ladies of Distinction. Shanita has received numerous awards and honors in recognition of her business, scholarly, civic, and community activities.

Happily married with two young sons, she credits her family with keeping her grounded. They are featured in the 2002 novel, "A Baby's Coming to Your House" by Shelly Moore Thomas.

To receive a free success strategy consultation or a complimentary copy of "The College Survival Guide" contact Shanita today at 773-416-0744 or email shanitaspeaks@sbcglobal.net • mailto:shanitaspeaks@sbcglobal.net

# Leadership Lessons Learned From Lucille Jones

Lucille Jones was my maternal great-grandmother. Born in 1898, she was a stout woman, wide in berth, with a shock of white hair that she wore in short braids placed in a neat crown around her head. She had skin the color of melted caramel, sharp grey eyes and a ready smile. In a word, she was a beauty.

In this chapter, I will examine the lessons conveyed in the kitchen, living room, and front porch of Lucille Jones or Great Grand, as I called her. I will examine the role this family matriarch played in formulating my voice as an African American woman and leader.

My initial ideologies about leadership were formed during our family's annual trip to Brinkley, Arkansas, a place I affectionately dubbed the 'mosquito resort of the south.' The highlights of my trip were my experiences with Great Grand, whose stories and life events greatly influenced my understanding of the world and what I thought my contribution would be. This is directly in accord with the idea proposed by Antoinette McDonald in her work entitled, "Everything I Needed to Know I learned In Big Mama's Kitchen" and Walter Fisher in his book, "Narration As a Human Communication Paradigm: The Case of Public Moral Argument," who states that human beings are "homo narrans," or storytellers.

> "The idea of human beings as storytellers indicates the generic form of all symbol composition; it holds that symbols are created and communicated ultimately as stories meant to give order to human experience and to induce

others to dwell in them to establish ways of living in common, in communities in which there is sanction for the story that constitutes one's life (Fisher, 6)."

Looking back, I realize that Great Grand's narratives were actually life lessons, assisting me in navigating my way through the world. With her "tell-it-like-it-'tis" flair, Great Grand's stories were always told with the intent of conveying some moral lesson, all of which I readily apply in my business and personal relationships today, particularly in the area of leadership. In this chapter, I will share six of those lessons with you, as taught to me by an extraordinary woman whose presence, though no longer seen, is always felt and whose teachings have become a part of me.

**Leadership Lesson #1: THE POWER OF CONFIRMATION**

*"I must undertake to love myself and to respect myself as though my very life depends on self-love and self respect."*
**—June Jordan, poet and civil rights activist**

Our arrival to Great Grand's white frame home was heralded by warm greetings, hugs and kisses bestowed on us from the front porch by a slew of uncles, aunts, cousins, and people simply claiming to be related to us. Throughout the entire gathering Great Grand would sit in her rocking chair that was positioned in the middle of the porch, smiling and taking it all in. The best part for me was all the compliments I received, which ranged from, "You're such a beautiful girl, look at those big pretty eyes!" "Watch out now, she's gonna break some hearts!" to "She's as smart as a whip, I tell you!" But the best compliment, which was always the same, came from Great Grand. "You have the mark of greatness," she would whisper. "You are going to do this family proud." "Ay-men!" the porch congregation would echo in agreement. According to McDonald, this language, "filled with rich, rhythmic innuendos and full-bodied sounds, is called 'talk-sing.' Often led by the matriarchal voices of the family, talk-sing is when the words are spoken, but some words are held out and sung, and often repeated back by participants, similar to a call and answer in the devotional portion of church service."

By the time I left the porch to enter the house, I was no longer walking, I was floating. The awkward, skinny adolescent had suddenly morphed into a pretty, smart young woman. Great Grand's words were transformative in nature, a confirmation that true leaders give others faith in themselves.

**Action Step:** Identify the person(s) in your life who inspires you to be your best self. If there are none, find them!

## Leadership Lesson #2: THE POWER OF CHOICE

> *"If you're hasty in making decisions, the next time you*
> *think you have all the information, stop and ask yourself,*
> *'Is that everything?'"*
> **—O Magazine, November 2002**

During our mandatory visit to the grocery store (Great Grand wanted to make sure her pantry was stocked with all the things we liked to eat) I would cajole her to purchase all the items my parents would never let me buy at home. One summer, I convinced her that no breakfast would be complete without two boxes of my favorite cereal (way too much for a four-day visit) and instant coffee. In my 12-year-old mind, the latter represented a special potion that appeared to magically transform adults, particularly my parents, from grumpy beings to happy campers after just one cup each morning. Now was my chance to have that experience. Euphoria!

Sometimes during our annual visits, my parents would cajole Great Grand into flying "north" to Chicago so that she could see the city. Each time they asked, Great Grand would and promptly retort, "If God had intended for me to fly, he would have given me wings."

Leaders make decisions on a regular basis. The question then becomes: Are they making principle-based decisions or ones based on the popular choice? The decision-making process of principle-driven leaders is shaped by the commitment to moral goals which shape their outlook and attitude. Thus they are able to take positive actions and feel good about those actions.

**Action Step:** What choices will you make, starting today, that will positively impact your personal life, and the lives of others in your organization and/or company?

**Leadership Lesson #3:**
**TAKE RESPONSIBILITY FOR YOUR OWN ACTIONS**

*"Each man must look to himself to teach him the*
*meaning of life. It is not something that is discovered,*
*it is something molded."*
**—Antoine de Saint-Exupery, French aviator and author**

The next morning, I gleefully sat down to breakfast that consisted of two bowls of Raisin Bran cereal (with extra sugar) and a cup of coffee (loaded with cream and again, sugar). After consuming this colonic nightmare, I had plenty of time to assess the lesson from this experience while running back and forth to the bathroom. This little 'dance routine' prevented me from going outside to play with my cousins and participating in the annual family talent show. Bummer! Editor's Note: I have not had a cup of coffee since.

There were many other instances where Great Grand's life lessons about personal responsibility crept into my conscious and subconscious mind. Most of these lessons were taught metaphorically, usually as she prepared some portion of the Sunday meal. For example, when I inquired how she knew exactly how much sugar to add to her "other side of heaven" mustard and collard greens without using a measuring spoon, she would exclaim, "Baby, when you've been cooking as long as I have the only measuring cup you need is right here." She would then illustrate this statement by cupping her weathered fingers into the shape of a small bowl. She continued, "But when I was a young woman, there were many times when I didn't get it exactly right, and your Great Grand daddy would laugh and say he couldn't tell if he was eating greens or grass. Chile, that hurt me so! But I kept at it, and it wasn't long before I knew exactly how much sugar them bitter ole collards needed to make 'em sing! Just like I know the same thing about you!" and she would giggle like a school girl as she grabbed me off the wooden stool standing at attention next to the stove and planted a big kiss on my forehead.

Remembering this adage has helped me deal with many challenges that I have faced in my personal and professional life. My version of the lesson is: If you make a mistake, own it, and keep working toward the desired outcome.

**Action Step:** All individuals, including leaders, make mistakes. But mistakes are often hidden opportunities for growth. Do you currently recognize your mistakes as hidden opportunities? If not, what will you do to shift that learning paradigm?

## Leadership Lesson #4: NO PAIN, NO GAIN

> *"It is not doing the things we like to do, but doing the things we have to do which causes growth and makes us successful. Success depends not merely on how well you do the things you enjoy, but how conscientiously you perform those duties you don't enjoy."*
>
> **—John C. Maxwell, Developing the Leader Within You**

One particularly grueling aspect of my summer visits was having Great Grand comb my hair, particularly after it had just been washed. It was as a brutal ritual that I likened to corporal punishment. The reason for this was due largely to the fact that I was "tender-headed," a term used in the African American community to refer to a woman or girl who needs special care and attention when having her hair styled. In other words, if you simply raked my head with a comb, I would let out a series of screams so loud, even the dogs and cats would seek cover. Needless, to say Great Grand would have none of that and, with me tightly secured between two legs that resembled sturdy tree trucks, she would comb my hair and "grease my scalp" until I was sporting a neatly corn-rowed hairstyle that would last our entire visit. Hallelujah!

This vignette illustrates what leadership guru John Maxwell refers to as a "play now and pay later or pay now and play later" scenario. In his book, Developing the Leader Within You, Maxwell states, "regardless of the choices, one thing is certain: Life will demand payment." Great Grand taught me this important discipline by making me sit still and have my hair braided. Once my hairstyle was complete, I could run and play with my cousins from the break of dawn until dusk. But whenever I didn't sit still long enough for the process to be completed, I would have to stay in the house every day and repeat the ritual of having my hair braided in sections. I only needed to face this scenario for several days before realizing that I needed to "pay up front" and allow Great Grand to braid my hair all at once.

This lesson has been so valuable to me that my husband, Jimmy, and I are teaching it to our sons, Jimi and Anthony. We want them to realize, early in life, that they will always have the power of choice. The sooner they learn to separate their desires from necessities, the more successful they will be.

**Action Step:** Everyday brings an opportunity to develop inner strength. What goals have you identified that require you to face certain challenges? What is today's challenge? How will you meet it?

**Leadership Lesson # 5:**
**WHEN IN DOUBT, CONSULT AN AUTHORITY**

*"It is easier to get up the hill when you climb it together."*
**—Ken Blanchard and Marc Muchnick,**
**The Leadership Pill**

During our summer visits we could count on the fact that our Sundays would be spent in church. Come rain, sleet, or shine my cousin Lakecia, my sister Danielle and I would be found sitting next to Great Grand who would sport a "church hat" cocked defiantly to the right side of her head in the front pew, her favorite spot. Whenever I would complain about the weather being too messy outside and the fact that the mud produced from the rain would ruin my "Sunday clothes and shoes," Great Grand would simply respond "God didn't stop making the world 'cause of a little rain," and that would end the conversation. I would then settle in to listen to one of the church choir's ground swelling musical selections, swinging my bobby-sock clad legs. Sometimes it felt like our church was being literally lifted off the ground once the choir got going!

In retrospect, what I learned from those Sunday sermons, beyond the minister's messages which were loaded with lots of saliva and salvation, has been an invaluable tool in my life. The primary lesson that I derived was that no matter how large the problem may appear to be, whether it is a demanding work project or family issue, it is imperative that you do not try to solve the problem alone. You must seek assistance from an outside source or higher authority.

**Action Step:** Who are key individuals or authority figures in your life that you can refer to for assistance or spiritual advising? What will you do to expand that network?

**Leadership Lesson #6:**
**BY INSPIRING OTHERS, YOU LEAVE A LEGACY**

> *"Life is not meaningful...unless it is serving an end beyond itself; unless it is of value to someone else."*
> **—Abraham Joshua Heschel, Jewish theologian**

Great Grand passed away in 1987, when I was in my early teens, a time when my attention was transitioning from Barbie dolls to boys. Her funeral was a simple one, much like the woman herself, and afterward the family gathered at her white frame home for fellowship. Somewhere during the hustle and bustle, as I consumed warm punch and cold chicken, I realized that my Great Grand had never told me she loved me. Not in exact words, anyway. It was also at that moment when I realized that she didn't need to, because it was evident in the flicker of her eyes, the gentle touch of her hands and the way she stirred her famous pot of collard greens. It was her retelling of the stories about her childhood, her marriage to my great-grand-father West, and her ability to raise eight children alone when he died. The writer Dorothy C. Fisher is quoted as saying, "A mother is not a person to lean on, but a person to make leaning unnecessary."

My great-grandmother was an individual who was not perfect, but who was guided by truth. She was a woman who gave of herself unconditionally, who loved and hurt deeply, and through the way she lived her life and shared her dreams and hopes, provided me with a precious "toolbox" of life lessons that can be applied to any situation. I, in turn, am sharing those lessons with you, so that you can benefit from them as well. In so doing, I am honoring the wisdom, spirit, and courage of our beautiful family matriarch, whose spirit is still guiding me today.

Once in a while, you have an experience that appears to affirm that life is in partnership with someone to teach you something. Great Grand gave voice to those spiritual lessons. I love you too, Lucille Jones. Continue to rest in peace.

**Action Step:** Take a moment to write down whose lives you touch or have the ability to touch in a positive way, starting today.

**Leadership Lessons Learned from Lucille Jones:**

*Leadership Lesson #1:* The Power of Confirmation

*Leadership Lesson #2:* The Power of Choice

*Leadership Lesson #3:* Take Responsibility for Your Actions

*Leadership Lesson #4:* No Pain, No Gain

*Leadership Lesson # 5:* When in doubt, Consult an authority

*Leadership Lesson #6:* By Inspiring Others, You Leave a Legacy

### SIX ACTION STEPS:

1. Identify key person (s) in your life who inspires you to be your best self. Write down the name (s) of that person (s). If there are none, find them!

_____

_____

_____

_____

_____

2. What choices will you make, starting today that will positively impact your personal life, and the lives of others in organization and/or company?

_____

_____

_____

_____

_____

3. All individuals, including leaders, make mistakes. But mistakes are often hidden opportunities for growth. Do you currently recognize your mistakes as hidden opportunities? If not, what will you do to shift that learning paradigm?

_____

_____

_____

_____

4. Everyday brings an opportunity to develop inner strength. What goals have you identified that require you to face certain challenges? What is today's challenge? How will you meet it?

_____

_____

_____

_____

_____

5. Who are key individuals, mentors, or authority figures in your life that you can refer to for assistance or spiritual advising? What will you do to expand that network?

_____

_____

_____

_____

_____


6. Take a moment to write down the names of those persons whose lives you touch or have the ability to touch in a positive way starting today.

_____

_____

_____

_____

_____

**Stephanie Durden**

Exciting…Electric…Versatile…Motivating …are just a few words that describe Stephanie Durden. She is multi-talented and is in high demand in the motivational speaking industry.

She is a dynamic combination of over 20 years of experience as a project manager for Fortune 500 Company- Eaton Electrical Corporation and as a professional speaker with Monster's Making It Count programs. She has reached and inspired over 125,000 high school and college students within the past two years providing interactive and exciting presentations which earn her "RAVING" reviews from students and guidance counselors.

Acting is also one of her passions. Within the past 10 years she has performed in leading roles on stage in productions- One Flew Over The Cuckoo's Nest, Mother's Love, The Best Little Whorehouse in Texas and Fences to name a few. Her credits also include Oprah Winfrey's ABC production, "The Wedding" starring Oscar winner Halle Berry. Her past experience provide lessons learned, success principles and humorous stories that audiences can feel.

Stephanie received her bachelor's degree from Fayetteville State University. She is a member of ToastMasters International and has served on numerous boards such as United Way Diversity Committee, Belk Teen Board, Vice-President of Big Brothers, Big Sisters and Smart Start Advisory Board.

Her mission in life is to empower and influence others to live to the maximum potential and be all that God has called them to be. As a wife to Aldvan and mother to Christian, she shares her generosity and loving spirit with her immediate family and Cumberland Christian Center Church family every day.

In the words of the late coach Paul "Bear" Bryant who was the winningest football coach in the history of major football when he retired from University of Alabama-

"If you believe in yourself, have dedication and pride and never quit, you'll always be a winner. The price of victory is high, oh but so are the rewards!"

**DURDENSTEPHANIE@AOL.COM**

**910-487-4702**

# Stepping Into Leadership

As I stood in the lightning and pouring rain,with my golf umbrella in Wilmington, North Carolina, I thought to myself, "either I am crazy or I must want this pretty bad". I stood there for about 3 hours with approximately 3500 other crazy people waiting for my chance to audition for the upcoming television mini series entitled "The Wedding" produced my Oprah Winfrey and staring Oscar winner Halle Berry. My once carefully curled hair and near perfect makeup had been ruined by the elements and I sure didn't feel like TV material. But something inside me would not allow me to give up. Once I was actually inside the studio, the long awaited audition process consisted of only reading a few lines while being videoed in front of a team of television experts. This couldn't have taken more than 1 minute. That's it-I said to myself. I couldn't believe it. That's it, I pondered to myself as I drove the 2-hrs home. I wondered if it was really worth it.

A few days later my fate was determined. I am notified by phone that I made it. It was worth it!!! "I AM IN." I share the good news with approximately 100 people consisting of friends, co-workers and family and we "all" begin to dream.

When most people hear the word "leader" they think of examples such as an officer of the law or military, a chancellor or professor of a university, a pastor of a church, a CEO of a major corporation or perhaps the President of the United States. Certainly, all of these are examples of leaders and deserve our respect, however we should not limit our list or our thinking to such positions, otherwise we limit ourselves and deny ourselves countless opportunities. The next 8 steps will direct and lead you systemically to become the leader you were created to be. This simple path of progression will show you how regardless of your current situation how you too can shape and mold the leader in you. Are you ready? Let's go.

## Step # 1
## Recognizing you are a leader.

*You must recognize that you are a leader.* This is the most important step to your development. I'll say it again. You ARE a leader. You are valuable and precious. You have gifts, and talents immersed deep within you waiting to be improved, perfected, discovered and shared. The question is what will you do with all your treasures and gifts. Think about it for a few seconds. Who are you currently leading with your talents? Is the path a positive, fruitful one or a negative, destructive one?

You actually have an opportunity to change your life as well as others using the gifts that have been given to you. From this day on when you look at a person, think in terms of numbers. Experts say that each person represents approximately 25 people. Each person representing a family. Sounds like a potential leader to me.

Maybe your gifts need developing and sharpening but they are there. They are there lying dormant within your spirit waiting to be activated. So what are you waiting for? Let's activate it!

**Before we move to Step #2 repeat this out loud 3 times-**

I AM VALUABLE AND PRECIOUS. THERE ARE GIFTS AND TALENTS INSIDE ME AND I RECOGNIZE TODAY, M/DAY/YEAR THAT **I AM A LEADER!!!!!** Repeat, Repeat

List three of your talents.

_____

_____

_____

Congratulations!!! You now recognize you are a leader and are ready to proceed to

## Step #2
## Developing a Leadership Mentality

*You must develop a leadership mentality.* Who do you think you are? Okay, ask the question again. This time when you ask the question place the emphasis on "you". Remember when you were in high school and a classmate or a so-called friend asked you that outlandish question. Perhaps you had a new hairstyle or had received an "A" on the Calculus test and you were feeling pretty great, but when you heard that question, it would stop you dead in your tracks. Your head would drop a few notches, your eyes would blink as if you were searching for new information and you immediately lost the strut in your step. You may have awaken that morning and gotten on the bus as a "10" but all of a sudden you feel like a "2". What happened? The hairstyle or the A grade didn't change but the way you felt about yourself certainly did. You allowed doubt and disbelief to enter your mind and alter your positive thoughts. This scenario continues to happen to us throughout our adult lives. Looking back at "The Wedding" audition, I could have easily quit before I got started. At the audition, as I looked around I saw many younger, thinner, more experienced actresses than myself and I wondered if I was wasting my time. The thought was there, but I didn't give in to those thoughts of "who do I think I am. Giving in would have meant forfeiting an awesome opportunity that I cherish to this day. It would have also denied many other people an opportunity to share in the experience.

You must believe in yourself. See yourself as God sees you, not how James, John or Leroy or Michelle, Cindy or Linda view you. They have no idea of how **GREAT** you are. How and what you think of yourself will determine what you will become. Start to think of youself as a leader by eliminating and eradicating any negative or doubtful thoughts that would prevent your from accomplishing your assignment.

## Step #3
## Changing Your Words

The words that you speak about yourself and your situation are powerful. Words can not only hurt but negative words can kill. They can kill your spirit and your dreams, preventing the leader in you from emerging. On the other hand positive words propel you in the right direction and are a springboard for success. Words are a direct result of our thoughts therefore Step #2 is paramount. The Bible compares the tongue to a rudder of a huge ship. Although the rudder is very small in size, it controls the direction of the entire ship. The tongue operates the same way. The tongue and the words you speak dictate the direction of your life. Think about that for a few seconds. Is your life going in the right direction??? You can change the course of your life just by changing the words you speak.

*Change your thoughts, change your words and change your world.*

Your words are like seeds which fall on fertile soil, forming root and developing and growing. Your words will either form death or life.

*Remember you are planting seeds.*

As a young girl we lived with my grandmother in a small town in North Carolina. Now she loved to work in her garden. I didn't. But because we lived in her house under her rules we had to rise early in the morning to work in the garden. So with my straw hat, dungarees and hoe in hand (just like her), I would plant tomato and cucumber seeds. We would regularly water and remove weeds from our expected harvest. It never failed that within a certain time period out of the dirt (earth) came the reddest, prettiest, juiciest tomatoes and picture perfect cucumbers. The fruit that we received was always based on the seeds we planted and words work the same way. Start to plant good words, positive words, words that will bring out the leader in you.

## Step #4
## Start today.

*Today matters, therfore start developing your plan today.* No more excuses and no more delays.

*In the words of the famous Les Brown-*

> *You don't have to be great to get started*
> *but you do have to get started to be great.*

Take one step at a time. Develop your plan. Write your plan down on paper. Start now. Write down 2 goals you would like to complete this year.

Use your planner to strategically plan how to achieve each goal.

Goal 1 _____

Goal 2 _____

## Step #5
## Raising Your Expectancy Level

*Expect it to happen.* I am sure you have heard the following phrase:

### Preparation + Opportunity= Success

This is so true. When preparation merges with opportunity success is inevitable. Get ready. Improve your skills. Rehearse. See yourself in action so that when it happens you are ready and prepared. Read and engage yourself with material related to your interest. Take classes or join organizations that will enhance your skills. Dream like you used to dream as a child before your develop those nasty negative thoughts.

**Dare to dream today and expect your dreams to become reality.**

Write down 2 things that you expect to happen. Based on the goals that you set for yourself in Step #4 write down things you expect to happen as a result of those goals.

*I expect* _____

_____

*I expect* _____

_____

## Step #6
## Start NetConnecting

*Surround yourself with people who think like you and bigger than you.* Invest your time in other people who have similar interests. Invest in a mentor or trainer. Face it- you can not do it alone. It is not meant for you to do it alone. You will need the advice and expertise of other people who have already run the race you are competing in. Stay focused on the prize. Invest in your goal-your time, your money. Looking back this was the one step that delayed my progress the most. It is said that experience is the best teacher. I strongly disagree. Take advantage of lessons learned from other people. Learn from others without enduring the pain, loss of time and/or money.

## Step # 7
## Making It Happen

*This is the step where everything comes together.* You can think about it, talk about it and plan it all out to a letter, but until you include this necessary ingredient it will never be complete. It's similar to having a new car in the garage but no gas in it. No fuel, no action. This ingredient is called "corresponding actions." Corresponding actions implies work and action. I believe this is the one ingredient that separates the winners from those who want to be winners. We all want to win, to lead, but are you willing to pay the price, are you willing to sacrifice the time, the money and do the work required to win, to lead.

A very familiar story of a leader is the story of Noah. You remember him don't you? We all read about Noah, the ark and the flood as a child. I encourage you to go back and review it again but this time as an adult. Look at the story from a leader's perspective. What if Noah had never added corresponding actions to this plan? What if he had just thought about what God told him to do, talked about it with his family and neighbors and just stopped there? Do you really think he would have built the ark (ship)? Absolutely not. Noah could have just waited for his ship to come in. After all, God being all-powerful could have just provided it. There are a lot of people sitting of the shore of life waiting for their ship to come in-waiting on the lottery ship, inheritance ship, who can I sue ship and on and on. They believe this ship (opportunity) will provide money, riches and will be the key to their happiness.

*But I challenge you today –*
*to stop waiting on your ship to come in and start building your ship.*

Noah was not a shipbuilder but everything he needed to get the job done was within him and the same is true for you. Noah not only led his family but he saved his family from a dying world. Who could you save by becoming the leader within you?

## Step # 8
## Helping Others To Become a Leader

*Dr. Martin Luther King Jr. once said the following quote-*

> *"Everybody can be great because anybody can serve.*
> *You don't have to have a college degree to serve. You*
> *don't have to make your subject and verb agree to*
> *serve. You only need a heart full of grace. A soul*
> *generated by love."*

This quote is still true today. So, if you want to be great just serve. Find ways to serve and give. Find ways to help others grow into the leader they were created to be. Give of yourself. If you are really honest with yourself someone probably did it for you. I know a lot of people sure did it for me and I am so thankful. Take a few seconds and write down the names of three people who have inspired and helped you in life. Give them a phone call or send them a card to say "thank you" just to let them know appreciate what they deposited in your life. It <u>will</u> be a Hallmark moment.

In conclusion, the leader in you is waiting to lead, to live and to love. Don't live by default, accepting any and everything that comes your way. Take charge of your life starting today by applying these 8 steps and watch your world go to a whole new dimension.

Stephen P. Duncanson

Stephen P. Duncanson is an acclaimed motivational speaker and dynamic trainer. Rapidly becoming known as "America's Voice of Motivation"–Steve is a native of New York and a veteran of the New York City Police Department, specializing in the areas of leadership and personal development. As President & CEO of True Destiny Communications, LLC., he is sought after as a speaker and trainer for corporations, non-profit organizations and educational institutions alike. His compelling stage presence, and mind-blowing delivery, create a potent message of business leadership and true personal empowerment. Steve is a member of the Les Brown Speakers' Network and impacts audiences around the globe.

**Steve Duncanson**
425 46th Street
Brooklyn, N.Y. 11210

Office: (631) 433-8413

Fax: (631) 271-9044

steveduncanson@aol.com

# The Balancer of Influence

When I was a kid, growing up on the streets of Brooklyn, New York, life was a daily adventure. The concrete jungle, as it has often been referred to, held many dangers for those unaware of how to navigate its landscape. It was the streetwise kid who knew that if you were to survive in the "neighborhood" you had to either learn to fight, learn to run, or develop alliances. Although I'd learned to be pretty good at the first two, (especially running) it was the last category that I had come to rely on the most; for safety as well as recreation.

For the most part, I got along very well with almost all the kids on the block, but the guys who I hung out with the most were my two next door neighbors, Malcolm and Robby. Although I was the oldest and tallest of the three, (which at that age kind of qualified me for leadership) we were relatively close in age and year or so apart in grade. So we had a lot in common. Very often I would, be able to influence the pace simply by reason of suggestion. Whether it would be what game or sport we would play, whose house we would hang out at or whose mother we should get to make us something to eat, my recommendations usually met with a favorable outcome. Though I may have made the suggestion, we all benefited as a result.

One summer however, a new "kid" named Papo, moved onto the block. Now Papo (whose real name I never learned) was a couple of years older and several inches taller than me, Malcolm and Robby. As such he represented an imposing presence among the rest of us and wasn't shy about letting us know it either. Given the aforementioned information and the fact that he lived just across the street and a few houses east of me, neither fighting nor running were viable options. So what was left in my ten year olds thinking was to develop an alliance. That we did; or so I thought.

Papo quickly established himself as the "leader" of our little group and bade us to do his bidding. Whatever he wanted to do, wherever Papo wanted to go, whatever he wanted us to say, that's what we did. And rarely was it really to our benefit. Not only would he intimidate us into making fun of the other kids on the block, thereby alienating ourselves from them, but he would subtly also sow seeds of distrust among the three of us. So much so that the fun we used to have together as a trio, had become a daily grind of competition for Papo's favor and approval.

It was only a matter of time before our parents noticed the change. Our dysfunction had begun to create a reputation for us in the neighborhood that represented the polar opposite of what they were attempting to instill in us. It was a conversation with my Dad (a meeting which he called, of course) that turned me around then and has since become the resonant tone that spurs me in the direction of greatness today. His specific words I don't recall as they were probably heard differently by me at ten years old. But the essence of his message I shall never forget. He said; "Stephen you will never become a leader until you wake up and realize that you already are one!"

Wow! I was totally mystified. What was this thing that he saw that I could not? Why would he tell me that I already am a leader? What did he know that escaped my consciousness?

It wasn't until years later that the sagacity of my Dad revealed itself as I was ironically drawn to the study of the topic of leadership. Through college, research, seminars, independent reading, and more I have come across many different definitions for what leadership is; from the technical to the philosophical. But no one definition so accurately and concisely captures its essence like the one expressed in a book called *"Developing the Leader Within You,"* by Dr. John C. Maxwell. In it he communicates the understanding quite succinctly that ***"leadership is influence; nothing more, and nothing less."***

There it was, in the simplest terms; "the person with the most influence IS the leader." End of story, period. What my father understood was that we each have the ability to influence the lives of others. Some to a greater, others to lesser a degree, but we all possess the capacity. Yet if we are unaware of the ability that we have to do so, there is no way for us to realize our *true destiny* in this area. There is no way that we will ever be able to unleash the leader that is within us.

The full working definition of leadership divined by Dr. Maxwell actually has two parts. The first declares that *"a leader is one who influences others to follow for a common cause or purpose..."* I share this belief with almost every audience I speak to on the topic of leadership. But often times the profundity of its understanding is missed, I believe, because of its subtlety. Influence has long been likened to an iceberg in that they are each 10% visible and 90% invisible. That being the case, there are many times when we are being influenced and we may not even realize it.

As a matter of fact, there is a whole genre of science dedicated to its study, called the Psychology of Persuasion. Dr. Robert Cialdini, a long time professor of psychology at Arizona State University, has spent years in the scientific investigation of the process by which people are influenced and reach their decisions. That study has led him to enumerate six social and psychological principles underlying the thousands of individual tactics that successful persuaders use everyday in order to gain compliance. Those principles are: The Rule of Reciprocity, Commitment and Consistency, Social Proof, Liking, Authority and Scarcity.

Now it is not my intention to breakdown the details of each of the aforementioned categories. However, I do wish to point out the fact that as you begin to examine the elements of each of the principles, you will notice that they are very simple. In other words, it doesn't take a proverbial rocket scientist to figure them out or more significantly, to apply them. You will see that they have deep roots into the understanding of human nature. They are strategies that can be and are utilized by anyone to increase the likelihood of gaining compliance or eliciting a desired response.

The point I want to drive home with the greatest emphasis is the fact that although influence may be subtle, it is extremely powerful. But if you don't recognize its power, you won't use it. You will find yourself in situations or even in positions of authority, with the ability to take action, yet fail to do so. You will find yourself complaining, blaming others or sitting around wishing (**W**-*aiting* **I**-*dlely* for **S**-*omething* to **H**appen) for someone else to do what you "could have" done.

Accepting the fact that "leadership is influence," concomitantly means that we each have a "response-ability" to grow in and develop our own. To recognize, realize and utilize the power and the subtlety of influence to create for those whom we lead, as well as ourselves, a desired reality. Embracing the understanding that all we have is what we are, but what we are can be enough. Enough, that is - to start. Continual growth is absolutely essential.

The issue of personal growth is something that operates at the very core of leadership. It not only represents the premier determining factor as to how far one can go as a leader, it stands as the ultimate mark of identification as to the quality of leader you are.

When I refer to personal growth, I'm not talking about the academic or even technical knowledge that the leader possesses. Now of course, being educated and knowledgeable in the field of ones endeavors is important. I would by no means discount the value of the need for intellectual competence in leadership. However, education is only an entry level platform of qualification for the position of leadership. More important than the **position of** leadership, is the **person in** the position.

Now, if the first part of the definition of leadership gives us a clear understanding of its essence, I believe that the second significantly ups the ante on what leadership is really all about. As a matter of fact, in my mind, it comes to represent the true line of delineation between good leaders and great leaders; between those that impress and those that impact; those who make a mark and those who make a difference. That full definition, as British Field Marshal Bernard Montgomery also defines it; leader: *"one who influences others to follow for a common cause or purpose – **and possesses the <u>character</u> which inspires confidence."** In other words (and reflecting the title of this chapter); character is the balancer of influence.

That's right. **The difference maker is character.** Webster defines it as "the combination of emotional, intellectual, and moral qualities that distinguishes an individual." As I searched through the myriad of academic and technical definitions, none seemed to make it as clear as the one taught to me in my youth. Again, simply stated; **character is who you are when no one is looking.** If I were to offer my own description today in the light of this topic of leadership, I would have to categorize it as the central nervous system or very backbone of what leadership is all about.

Now, before I go any further, there is both a disclaimer as well as a distinction that I need to make here. First the disclaimer; when I talk about character in leadership, I'm certainly not talking about being a "perfect" individual. Possessing character as a leaders is not about perfection. As a matter of fact, it's just the opposite. It's about being honest about your imperfection. It's acknowledging that you have flaws and being willing to do what's necessary to correct them as opposed to making excuses for them. It's a willingness to hold yourself to the same (or more often, to even greater) standards of responsibility and accountability as those whom you lead. It's about disclosure, not concealment; transparency, not opacity; consistency, not incongruity.

I've had occasion to work in organizations where the leadership would rather the atmosphere be like that of the ruler in the children's story of The Emperor's New Clothes. Where the monarch, knowing full well that his "flaws" were hanging out, expected everyone else to pretend that they didn't see what they really saw. When in actuality, all they saw is what really was; that being the "naked truth" about their ruler. When it comes to the issue of character in leadership, I believe Benjamin Franklin was right when he said that; "the key to success is to be in reality that it is that we would have others think ourselves to be."

The second matter that I hope to make clear is that of the distinction between character and personality. Often times the words are used synonymously, but in the case of the topic of leadership, I believe that they are very different.

The study of human personality development can be traced back hundreds of years. From early astrologers and their belief in the twelve signs that influenced behavior; to Hippocrates and his description of four the four temperaments – Choleric, Phlegmatic, Sanguine, and Melancholy; to the discussion of their variations by Dr. Jung in his book, "Psychological Types"; not to mention the Freudian model of the ego, superego and the id; Dr. Thomas Harris and his Transactional Analysis theory, the list goes on and on.

When you think about an individual's personality, you think in terms of assessing if the person is outgoing or shy; are they high strung or easy going; quick to act or cautious thinkers? These are all descriptions that give us better insight into how a person will act most of the time. Essentially, your personality **describes how** you are.

When you think about an individual's character however, you think more in terms of assessing whether they are honest and trustworthy? Do they have integrity, patience, perseverance, humility? These words lend themselves more to discovering the core of their being. Effectively, your character **defines who** you are. Simply stated; *personality describes "how" you are; character defines "who" you are.*

Heraclites, the Greek philosopher said that; "character is our fate...eventually we will only have what our character allows." Orison Marden said; "character is the indelible mark that determines the only true value of all people and their work." The volumes of study on leadership are replete with references to the absolute necessity of character. It is clearly the premier element that any truly successful leader cannot be without.

There's one other observation that I'd like to highlight about the difference between character and personality. Think about this; **you can fake your personality, but you can't fake your character.** Oh, you may be able to disguise it for a short period of time. There are a myriad of training programs in the marketplace that attempt to teach people how to control themselves, act properly and put there best foot forward. But let someone step too hard on that foot. "Aaaah, suki suki"! It's on now! The irrefutable truth is that character has an espial nature; its exposure is inevitable. Given the element of time and the proper circumstances, who you really are is going to come out.

That fact having been established, you've probably heard it said before that; "what makes you laugh, will also make you cry." Well, that very paradox operates in the realm of character development as well. The same factor that ultimately reveals character, is the very one that is needed in order to strengthen and develop character within us. Like all substances of great value; gold, diamonds, even pearls, character can only be can built through some process of adversity. Whether by friction, fire or force, the laws of nature, as well as the annals of history support the fact that adversity is the precipitator of both greatness and ruin. A leader's ability to handle pressure is one of the truest tests of their leadership capacity.

When discussing this aspect of leadership or even personal development, I often use the analogy of weight lifting or as it's known in the health & fitness industry, "resistance training." The reason that analogy works so well is because its application is universal. Every one of us can identify with both the challenges of lifting a heavy weight as well as the benefit that can be derived from doing so. It is the ability and decision to push against the weight that produces the desired result of muscle development. **Strength is not developed by success; it's developed by struggles.**

Similarly, the only way in which character can be developed is if we step outside of our comfort zone and challenge ourselves to do the difficult things. The more we exercise our muscles of honesty, integrity, reliability, patience and the like, the greater the corresponding level of both our capacity to lead and our value in the marketplace.

I always thought it interesting as I studied those men and women throughout history who we would categorize as successful, that in almost every case, the greatness for which they'd come to be known came after their many storied struggles. Generals after wars, politicians after defeats, activists after beatings and arrests; I could go on and on. The single cord that connects each and everyone whom we recognize today as great leaders is their ability to have withstood the character building tests of adversity. Each of them was _defined_ through the process.

The laws of the universe support the fact that "balance is the key to life." That is a virtually inviolate truth we have been taught to observe and respect for most of our lives. From the ballpark to the boardroom, there is the expectation that we be dealt with, with fairness and equity; especially when it comes to the issue of leadership. A strong sense of character practiced by the individual leader creates a kind of self governing that brings about that balance. As long as that leader is further, willing to submit to authority himself and be held accountable for his actions, he will have established the equipoise necessary for the proper utilization of influence.

Oh yeah, by the way, some of you may be wondering; "whatever happened to Papo from the old neighborhood?" Well, I wish I could tell you something dramatic or profound, like how Malcolm, Robby and I finally came to our senses, took courage and confronted our oppressive leadership, resulting in the end to his reign of terror and the subsequent liberation of our neighborhood. But that would be um…er…ahh…less than truthful. Quite honestly, a year or two later Papo moved away; never to be seen or heard from again. His departure brought on a celebration, much like the one experienced by the citizens of Munchkin Land at the demise of the Wicked Witch of the West in the story of The Wizard of Oz. I guess you can say that in the end, he went the way of all leaders with poor character – he left a mark, but never made a difference. How about you?

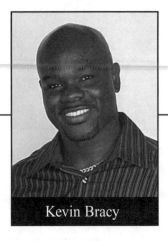

Kevin Bracy

Kevin has delivered messages for organizations such as 24 Hour Fitness, Hewlett Packard, SBC, Cal Trans, and Colonial Life Insurance. He has also enjoyed speaking to over 300,000 high school and college students across the country and has been privileged to speak at the T.D. Jakes Megafest Conference two years in a row. Kevin takes the opportunity to touch lives very seriously, he speaks on the subjects of motivation, leadership, diversity, overcoming obstacles, goal setting and change.

Kevin learned the importance of nurturing dreams at an early age after overcoming a difficult childhood. Despite his early life challenges, Kevin went on to earn a baseball scholarship to the University of Utah, acquired three college degrees, played two years of professional baseball in Canada and is now a successful speaker and entrepreneur.

Currently, Kevin runs a coaching program for professional speakers that spans across the United States as well as the United Kingdom. Within one year he helped thirty-one speakers become authors while writing two books of his own, The Top 10 Tips For Teen Success and 1 Little Idea Can CHANGE Your Life. Kevin has read and researched over 1,000 books on leadership, communication, sales and peak performance and has built a successful networking team, leading hundreds of independent business owners through the daily challenges of business ownership.

You can reach Kevin through his award-winning web-site: **www.kevinbracy.com**, by e-mail at **kevin@kevinbracy.com** or by phone at **877.210.2676**.

# Brace Yourself...13 Tips From a Leader's Perspective

Success in any company, team or business begins and ends with leadership. Have you ever wondered why a sports team that has a bad month or a bad year fires the coach rather than the players? It all comes down to leadership. It is an important subject in our world today, we are starving for world leaders we can believe in and put our trust in. Over the next few pages we will be discussing some ideas about effective leadership, the **BRACE YOURSELF** way. So get your footing, strap on your seatbelt and brace yourself for leadership success! Let's Roll!

## 1. Believe...We First, Not Me First

Leaders believe in the mindset of Mother Theresa who said, "I can do great things, you can do great things, but together we can change the world." They understand the concept, <u>individuals grow, but teams explode</u>. Leaders have a sixth sense about the fact that a community of people moving in the same direction with the same purpose is significantly more productive than an individual with direction and purpose. Leaders not only understand these facts, they also know that someone has to lead; they are willing to take on such a responsibility.

## 2. Read Daily

Not all readers are leaders, but all leaders are readers. Reading gives leaders what Anthony Robbins calls, "The Edge;" it enables them to get an inside perspective from the mindset of people who are successful leaders throughout our world. To lead one must read, notice the testimonials on books, leaders of the world write them. <u>Leaders know that by reading they can learn in 15 minutes what it took someone 15 years to learn</u>. Leaders like to speed up their learning curve by reading every chance they get.

### 3. Attitude Check!

**Leaders must check their attitude at the door.** Why? Because they know that their aura, charisma and energy is contagious, they get what they give. Leaders understand that in order to be productive and be able to fulfill the vision of the team, the temperature of the environment must be conducive to **Progress**! They know that attitude is the inner you expressed by the outer you; therefore, leaders frequently check their attitudes. Question: When was the last time you made a conscious, deliberate, determined, decision to give yourself periodic attitude checks throughout your day?

### 4. Crystallized Aim

To have crystallized aim means to pay more attention to detail. Walt Disney said, "make detail your top billing." The detail I am talking about is in your effort, making sure every effort is focused on attaining the goal at hand…minimizing any wasted effort. I like Brian Tracy's method that instructs those reaching for a goal to write it down 3 times a day to be sure it is on the front of their mind, the tip of their tongue and the top of their priority list.

In order to crystallize their aim, leaders are extremely aware of the three questions that need to be answered in order to be a successful and effective leader.

1. What are you really aiming for?
2. Why are you aiming for this?
3. How are you going to get there?

By answering these questions, a leader can be certain that "the unit" continues to aim in the correct direction at all times.

### 5. Edify Everyone

You may have heard the saying, "as the tide rises all ships rise." This is a very accurate statement. Leaders understand this and know that the art of edification is a powerful tool that some of the most successful leaders use in helping those around them rise to the occasion.

Dexter Yager is a man who built the largest network marketing team known to the world today, his network is made up of millions of people who have voluntarily decided to be part of his business team. He credits his massive success to his discovering the art of edification. He is truly the master of building up those around him up, encouraging them and pointing out their strengths, edification. Les Brown said, "love and happiness are perfumes, you can't sprinkle on others without getting some on yourself." Leaders build up those around them, in return their project, idea, and business prospers.

## 6. YOU Are The Example

What you are doing speaks so loud I can't hear what you are saying. What a leader says goes deeper in the psyche of the people they are leading when their actions are in harmony with their words. Effective leaders know that they are the ones laying out the vision, developing the plan of attack, and working out the phases in which the goals are to be achieved. They must always remember that they are the example that the team is watching, it is on them to set the pace and lead the pack, no matter what challenges or obstacles they are faced with.

Michael Jordan was one of the greatest athletes of all time; however, he was an even better leader. I remember watching a Sports Center piece which explained how he used to get upset at his teammates for not working hard during practice. His teammates said that Michael treated every practice as if it was an actual game, he took his practice regime very seriously. By watching Michael Jordan, his teammates grew to value practice and treat it in the same manner that he did…he led by example.

## 7. Observe A Mentor

Leaders aggressively study other leaders, they have a mutual sense of respect and know that they can learn something from everyone, whether it be through books, audios, or on a personal level. All of the leaders that I have ever studied such as Les Brown, Mark Victor Hansen, Dexter Yager, Ken and Joan Westenskow, Dennis and Sharron Delisle, my high school baseball coach, my chiropractor, all attribute much of their success to a mentor or mentors that they studied or observed.

My motto is "learn it, do it, then teach it!" If you never learn it then you will never get to the point of legitimately teaching it. The way you learn it is through someone who can teach you through their experience. Find a mentor to observe, it will shorten your learning curve.

## 8. Under Promise, Over Deliver

Successful leaders understand the importance of credibility; being a person who follows through on their word. They are conscious of making promises that they cannot keep and work hard to not bite off more than they can chew. A leader realizes that one episode of over promising and under delivering can destroy their credibility. <u>There is power in doing more than you have promised</u>, it creates a sense of trust and results in increased productivity, increased sales and positive attitudes.

## 9. Relationship Driven

Leaders who get major results on their campus, in their business or on their team are driven to establish relationships with their associates. They understand to get the most productivity out of a teammate, they must know what makes them tick, to know what makes them tick they must first relate *(root word of relationships)*. <u>People will work harder to fulfill a vision for leaders that they know, like and trust</u>; therefore, to be driven or guided to establish strong relationships is a must for any leader seeking to create momentum for their campus, business or team.

## 10. Speak With Direction, Authority and Confidence

When leaders speak people listen!! Why? Because leaders speak with direction…their conversation has reason behind it, they are not just speaking a bunch of meaningless empty words. Leaders know what they are saying, why they are saying it and what they want to accomplish through their words. They begin their conversations with an end in site. Leaders also take the time to get to know the audiences they are dealing with, to ensure that their message has an impact on those that are receiving it. When a true leader speaks confidence is created throughout the audience, they can relax and know that they have a leader that will lead them to the finish line.

When a leader speaks they are "The Authority" on the subject that they are discussing, they manifest their authority through their conviction, their passion and how they annunciate their words. When a leader speaks they create an atmosphere of total knowledge, meaning they speak as if they are the greatest resource of information on the specific topic or subject they are addressing. They dress the part, their gestures show their confidence and they walk as if they know where they are going…and they do.

There are certain people that when they walk into the room, the room brightens up, then there are others that when they leave the room the room brightens up. Leaders have the charisma and confidence that manifests itself the minute they enter a room, before they utter a single word. The type of energy that exudes from a leader is the invisible stuff that gets people to follow, it stems from confidence, posture and a sense of pride in themselves and the knowledge they possess. It is important to point out that a true leader is not big headed, they do not feel the need to put themselves on a pedestal, they get much of their confidence through lifting up and edifying those they work with.

I remember meeting Les Brown for the first time, I studied his body language, how he would meet and greet people, shake their hands, listen, speak with authority, look people in their eyes. I recall thinking what amazing energy he had, he spoke with conviction, authority and exuded confidence, all traits that have made him a man people have listened to and followed for over 20 years.

## 11. Energy, Energy, Energy

I read it in the book *The Power of Full Engagement* and it has stuck with me ever since, it said, "The number of hours in a day are fixed, but the quantity and quality of energy available to us is not, it is our most precious resource." The more we take responsibility for the energy we bring into this world, the more empowered and productive we become. The more we blame external circumstances the more negative and compromised our energy is likely to be.

Leaders understand how contagious energy is, be it positive or negative. It seems as though negative energy is more common than positive energy these days; therefore, true leaders know they must make a conscious, deliberate, determined effort to seek out the positive energy and transfer it into their teams for maximum results.

## 12. Life Long Learning

Most successful leaders have a daily success regime, a personal development regimen (PDR), which helps them raise the opinion they have of themselves and keeps them in a continual learning mode. By disciplining themselves to follow a daily regimen they slowly replace the self doubt we all struggle with and become an <u>example to those they lead</u>.

People with a high level of personal mastery live in a continual learning mode, they never arrive! The secret is incorporating your PDR into your DAILY life. The PDR consists of the following five things:

1. **Read** 15-20 minutes a day from something uplifting, empowering and positive on leadership.

2. **Listen** to no less than one audio on something uplifting, empowering and positive on leadership.

3. **Associate** with uplifting, empowering and positive leaders daily. Make it a daily practice to associate with people who are doing what you want to do, how you want to do it, at a level in which you want to do it.

4. **Mentorship** is vital, having a daily conversation with a mentor that is where you aspire to be in your field keeps your aim precise and will help you stay on track.

5. **Personal Exercise Program (PEP)** consisting of resistance training, cardiovascular exercise 3 times a week, supplementation, and a stretching routine will increase your energy as well as improve the way you feel about you. In order to succeed in any endeavor the most important factor is **YOU**.

## 13. Finish in Phases

Most leaders are visionaries, they see beyond the horizon, they are future oriented and pride themselves on being forward thinkers. There are times where every leader can get bogged by down by having such a BIG vision. Why? Because they are so focused on the future that they forget the phases necessary to get there. Experienced leaders know that there will always be projects in motion and no worthwhile project can be done overnight; therefore, to move into the future in an organized fashion while keeping their sanity it is important that projects are finished in phases.

**EXAMPLE:**
> Phase 1 of Project A
> Phase 2 of Project A
>
> Phase 1 of Project B
> Phase 2 of Project B

Phases are benchmarks along the road to completion.

You now have the 13 tips from a leaders perspective that will help you become an _effective leader_. In order to get the most out of these tips you must understand that information _without_ application leads to fascination; however, information _with_ application leads to transformation. Use these tips to transform your thinking and **unleash the leader you have within you!**

James Malinchak

James Malinchak has delivered over 2,200 motivational presentations at conferences and meetings worldwide, was featured in *Personal Branding* magazine, and was named Consummate Speaker of the Year by *Sharing Ideas* professional speakers' magazine. He has appeared in *USA Today, The Wall Street Journal* and several hundred other publications.

James began his sales career right out of college as a stockbroker with a major Wall Street Investment Firm and was awarded Most Outstanding Performance (twice) and #1 in New Account Openings (twice). While in his twenties, James became a partner in a company that handled the investments for many famous entertainers, authors and professional athletes.

Currently, James owns three businesses, has authored ten books, and has read and researched over 1,500 books on personal and professional development. He is a Contributing Author to, and serves as Associate Editor for, the #1 New York Times Best-selling book series *Chicken Soup for the Soul®*, with his own personal stories published in *Chicken Soup for the Teenage Soul, Chicken Soup for the Kid's Soul* and *Chicken Soup for the Prisoner's Soul.* James is the Co-Author of the upcoming book, *Chicken Soup for the Athlete's Soul.*

**James Malinchak · PO Box 530061 · Henderson, NV 89012**
**(888) 793-1196 · JamesMal@aol.com · www.Malinchak.com**

# Successful Leaders Are Master Networkers

"Why networking?" The answer is simple. It's not a coincidence that hundreds, even thousands, of people are hired for leadership positions over individuals more qualified and more experienced, merely because they have cultivated relationships with key centers of influence. It's not a coincidence that politicians are elected into office because they have cultivated relationships with more individual voters than their competitors. Through networking you will receive invitations that will expand your current knowledge base. Through networking you will be put in positions to expand your current skills and learn to communicate at many levels.

*Networking is communicating with others to create quality, mutually beneficial relationships.*

People often confuse networking with quantity of contracts. For the leader, this concept of networking defeats its very purpose-to enhance your cause or whose cause you can help to advance. Think of networking in terms of opening doors to the unknown. You might be tempted to believe the more doors that you have, the greater the odds you will make the right kinds of connections, right? Wrong. Networking is intentional by design. By placing yourself in situations that attract others with whom mutually beneficial relationships can be established, you increase the potential payoffs. Therefore, one of the greatest traits of the networking leader is their ability to actively identify what doors to open – not just how many doors.

Successful networking, however, also involves making something out of chance. Specifically, taking a coincidental encounter and fostering it into a mutually beneficial relationship is a networking characteristic that often gets over looked for a variety of reasons. Maybe the benefits aren't always obvious-or seem too far from your current scope of responsibility or reality. But, as I've learned from personal experience, you just never know. You need to overcome any fears or limiting beliefs that prevent you from taking advantage of chance encounters and have faith in the potential long term, as well as, short term benefits of your efforts. Consider the true story below.

Chances are you will run into someone of national celebrity once or twice in your lifetime. What you decide to do with that meeting is a reflection of the significance you put on networking. Do you ask for an autograph? Do you ask for a photo opportunity? Or do you remind yourself of the many values of networking? You will not always know how meeting someone of national exposure can possibly be an advantage to your role as leader. However, I learned how when I was presented with an opportunity to meet a famous author.

## In the Company of Fame

Several years ago, when I was working as a full-time stockbroker, I received a call from a client named Cynthia. She and her husband, Michael, are movie writers and they had been in Cape Cod, Massachusetts for a few weeks working on a movie. They were turning a book written by Mary Higgins Clark in to a made for television movie. Cynthia invited my business partner Jase and I to visit with them for a few days on the Cape. She also said Mary had invited us to attend a private dinner party she was hosting at her house. I naturally accepted despite the fact that when I put down the phone I asked Jase, "Who is Mary Higgins Clark?"

To take advantage of opportunities that may or may not result from encounters with an author, for instance, you need to minimally know something about their work. You would ideally also like to know about their background, how they came to be a writer, and where they get their inspiration to write. Since we were scheduled to leave for the Cape only a few days later, I was forced, as you often will be, to do my homework quickly.

**Networking Development Tips**

*Tip #1 – Do Your Homework*

Because planning is a component of networking, you will need to make lists and seek out resources that can answer basic questions about the person or individuals you will be meeting. Some information will be more difficult to locate, but if you are willing to put in the time, you can learn what you need to about someone to make a good first impression. For instance, who knows the same person you are trying to meet? Who else works with this person? Where do they live? I'm not suggesting you stalk your potential pool of networking targets, rather you sit down and list what information might help increase the quality of your potential interactions.

Despite the many possible ways of learning more about my famous upcoming dinner host, time required that I select only a few methods of learning about Mary Higgins Clark. Step one was a trip to my local bookstore-a place of great networking resources. I asked the person working behind the counter if she had ever heard of an author Mary Higgins Clark. She replied, "Oh yes," as she pointed to a display holding over ten of her books. Now I felt anxious. Despite my desire to read what appeared to be stacks upon stacks of her best-selling novels, I purchased only three to read on the plane. As I left the bookstore, I found myself less anxious and more excited about my upcoming encounter with such as established writer.

*Tip #2 – Take the Initiative and Introduce Yourself*

When meeting someone of notoriety, it is normal to act nervous to be concerned about making a bad first impression – despite your own level of success. However, even the most charismatic individuals say the wrong things out of nervousness or excitement. I think it's always wise to go for politeness. This seems like an obvious suggestion until you mistakenly call someone by their first name after a two-minute intro-duction. Whether the person you are approaching is famous or not, it's always acceptable to ask, "How would you like to be addressed?" after introducing yourself. I also like to have a few questions in mind that begin with the phrase, "Tell me about..." followed by a reference to something I know about the person, Because most people like to talk about themselves, the more the conversation places emphasis on who you are meeting–not why they should be thrilled to meet you–will most likely result in another encounter.

Fortunately, I didn't have to make any decisions about how to approach my dinner host, since Mary Higgins Clark greeted us as we approached her home. Still outside, Jase, Mary and I talked about a host of topics from our families and hobbies to the stock market. She was very interested in the market. She asked questions that, frankly, were rather complicated to answer. Instead of trying to impress her, a behavior mistakenly made by many trying to make a good impression, I employed a networking communication strategy of keeping it simple. So, we responded to her questions with simple, easy-to-understand answers.

### Tip #3 – Make it About Them

As suggested above, you never want to try to make yourself sound better, smarter, more knowledgeable (even though you might be) than your part-ners in conversation. When you do this you come off as condescending, and despite your desire to build a foundation for additional interaction, you may have just closed the door. In fact, it is often your goal to ask more questions than you answer. Keep the other person engaged in the conversation by having them share information about themselves. Despite your position of leadership or status, find a common ground of interest. Lastly, do what is needed to make yourself appear approachable. Asking if it's alright to offer your business card is just one way to ensure this happens.

Much to my delight, my use of effective networking skills with Mary Higgins Clark was immediately rewarded. This does not always happen. In fact, some encounters represent the start and the end. For whatever reason, the attempt to follow-up and continue the relationship doesn't result in an on-going relationship. However, you'll never know unless you immediately begin making a more conscious effort to reach out. Because I have tried to make the skills and attitudes mentioned above part of my personality, I am particularly thrilled when there is an immediate result. For example, as Jase and I were leaving after a wonderful evening of conversation over a New England dinner, Mary asked if she could talk to us for a minute. We walked with her to the corner of the room where she said, "I really like you guys and how easily you explained the answers to my questions. I'm looking to open another investment account with another company and I'd like to open the account with you."

## Tip #4 – Stay in Frequent Contact

Mary, and her family, are still clients to this day and have become very good friends. Why? We took the initiative to stay in contact and follow-up with her. There are many ways you can do this as a leader. Writing thank you cards, sending holiday greetings, sending articles of interest with a note or remembering events of significance with flowers, are all examples of how to stay in frequent contact. Sending an e-mail message-although impersonal compared to a letter-also keeps your name and contact information out there. Call certain contacts periodically and if you happen to be in their area take them to lunch or at least give them a quick call to say hello. Effective leaders recognize the importance of staying in touch with those in their network.

## Staying in Contact with a Childhood Friend

Let me give you another example of the payoffs of following up and staying in touch by telling you about a childhood friend. Michael and I played sports together in junior high school. After high school graduation our goals led us in separate directions. Mine led me to play college basketball in Ohio and Hawaii. Michael's goals led him to Detroit, where he began to train for a career as a professional boxer. We had not seen each other for several years but I stayed in touch with him. After graduating from college, I began my career as a stockbroker in Los Angeles.

One day, I picked up a local newspaper and I read the following headline: "Evander Holyfield to Defend the World Heavyweight Boxing Title Against Michael Moorer." I couldn't believe it! This was my childhood friend. Immediately, I called a mutual friend of ours back in our small hometown of Monessen, Pennsylvania to ask if he knew how to get in touch with Michael because the fight was taking place the following week in Las Vegas. He did and gave me the telephone number to the room of one of Michael's bodyguards. I left a message and asked if would have Michael return my call. Truthfully, I didn't think he would return my call because we hadn't seen each other for several years. Shortly thereafter, my telephone rang and it was Michael. He said he hadn't realized I was living in Los Angeles. More importantly, he said it was nice to hear from an old friend who stayed in touch all these years. He asked if I was planning on attending the fight. When I told him I would be there, he said to call him when I arrive so we could hopefully see each other.

To make a long story short, the night before the heavyweight title fight that would be broadcast to millions of viewers worldwide, I spent a few hours visiting with Michael in his hotel room. Since then, I have attended most of his fights and visited with him at the various training camps before each fight. Why? Simply because I took the initiative to stay in touch with someone I met in junior high school. If you are not making an effort to stay in touch with your contacts, then you could be missing many opportunities.

### Tip #5 – *Look for Ways to Offer Praise*

Making others feel good is essential for walking through doors once they have been opened. Congratulating someone for their accomplishments or thanking them for taking the time to speak with you, are ways to praise. This does not mean you act like a crazed fan, rather you think about what you could say that would make the other person feel good about themselves. Praising your own accomplishments can lead to a competitive tone in your conversations. Having a calm sense of self while praising others makes you appear self-confident and much more worthy of additional contacts.

### A Child Speaks Volumes

Recently, I was speaking in San Antonio, where my cousin, Davy Tyburski, lives. It had been several years since we had seen each other. Therefore, the invitation to stay at his house rather than in a hotel was warmly received. This would also give me a chance to visit with his wife and kids.

The night of my talk, Davy asked if he could bring his nine-year-old-son, Kevin, because he wanted to begin exposing him to things that could be helpful to his future success. Naturally I agreed. However, I mentioned that Kevin probably wouldn't be able to relate to most of the information. Davy understood but wanted his son to attend nonetheless.

For about 90-minutes, I spoke about how to create a powerful network of contacts. One of the main points I emphasized was the importance of making others feel good about themselves. Among the variety of suggestions was to simply take the time to leave a note for someone praising them for something they did that day.

After the talk, Davy, Kevin and I stayed another hour and a half so that I could answer questions and autograph books. Needless to say, it was now about 11:00 p.m. and past Kevin's bedtime. As a matter of fact, I noticed that Kevin was sleeping while I was answering questions and signing books. He continued to sleep on the ride home and as Davy and I helped him to his bedroom.

The next morning, I got out of bed and prepared to take a shower. As I opened the bedroom door, something caught my eye. A note with my name on it was taped to the door. It said, "Dear Cousin James, I just wanted to let you know that you did great last night. I can't wait to see you when I get home from school. Love, Kevin." Wow! I couldn't believe it! Kevin's simple gesture made me feel great and he motivated me to make an effort to leave more and more notes for others. If a nine-year old can take such initiative to praise, grown leaders can certainly do the same.

**Final Words**

No successful leader has achieved their goals without the assistance of others. It doesn't matter how knowledgeable, qualified, or experienced you are, without the assistance of others, you will most likely not excel. Networking can create a spider web effect by connecting you to opportunities. To lead effectively, you will need to stretch outside your immediate comfort zone to seek different ideas and discover a world of potential opportunities for yourself and your organization

It doesn't matter how much leadership experience you have or what your leadership qualifications are, if you aren't focusing on creating quality, mutually beneficial relationships, others may not be receptive to your ideas.

Mastering the art of networking will enhance your leadership abilities and opportunities.

## CHAPTER SUMMARY

- Being an effective leader requires expanding the quality of your contacts.
- You often never know the value of an initial interaction.
- It takes intentional thought to be an effective networker.
- Your first impression will determine how many additional interactions follow, but not always.
- There are five strategies that will enhance your abilities to become a master networker.